3, 136

For Carmen and Kathleen

Cogswell, Fred, 1917-
    A Long Apprenticeship

(Fiddlehead Poetry Books ; 303)

I. Title   II. Series.

PS8555.036L66   C811'.54   C80-094350-3
PR9199.3.C625L66

ISBN. No. 0-86492-000-8

A LONG APPRENTICESHIP;

THE COLLECTED POEMS
OF
FRED COGSWELL

Fiddlehead Poetry Books, 1980

VALLEY-FOLK

O narrow is the house where we are born,
And narrow are the fields in which we labour,
Fenced in by rails and woods that low hills neighbour
Lest they should spill their crops of hay and corn.
O narrow are the hates with which we thorn
Each other's flesh by gossip of the Grundies,
And narrow are our roads to church on Sundays,
And narrow too the vows of love we've sworn.

But through our fields the Saint John river flows
And mocks the patterned fields that we enclose;
There sometimes pausing in the dusty heat
We stretch cramped backs and lean upon our hoes
To watch a sea-gull glide with lazy beat
To wider regions where the river goes.

ROSE

Here in our town she bloomed, a scarlet rose
Among the other girls, and all the men
Who ever looked went crazy for her then,
Like bees that haunt the place where honey grows.
But when she left to dance in burlesque shows,
As shifty as the snow across the track
Of deer, the rumours of her life blew back,
Though what the wind that blew them no one knows.

And slowly to us boys and girls her case
Became a legend of iniquity ;
So when her father died and Rose came back
We watched with awe and curiosity
A thin, tall scare-crow dressed in faded black
With tears that trickled down her withered face.

ELLEN WARING

A fruitful tree of life is Ellen Waring ;
Where others of her kind bear when they suit,
She pays her husband's toil with yearly fruit,
Firm-fleshed as flesh from which it takes its faring.
But now her once-smooth skin in spots is wearing
Rough bark that only hands of death can smooth ;
Her trunk and limbs grow gnarled and stout to prove
The tree that bears must pay the price of bearing.

She is not so unto her husband's sight.
The light through which he sees is filtered by
The colours of one warm September sky
When she, on their first morning of delight,
Stood bare in limbs' and body's symmetry,
As lissom-lovely as a poplar tree.

HONOUR LOGAN

When to the prim, white house once more I came,
She met me at the door, then took my hand
Coolly in hers without a tremor, and
Gave me, as pure and proper as her name,
Such greetings as a friend of hers should claim.
Her skin was fresh and tender as a quince ;
How old she is I do not know, for since
I've known her she has always looked the same.

Still like a silk coccoon she keeps her form
Inside a veil of smooth, self-woven thread
Whose gloss defies the touch of sun and storm,
And those who see her never guess she grew
Bright wings of love one time that almost flew
Before a puff of gossip froze them dead.

HELEN GOODCHILD

Big-boned was Helen, but her eyes were warm
And bright with welcome when she'd ask us in ;
She had a smile that never would wear thin
And a clean brightness that no years could harm.
She helped her brother with his chicken farm
And kept his farmhouse sweet as new-made bread,
But no man liked her quite enough to wed,
Though all were conscious of her buxom charm.

She loved to feed the chickens one day old
That round the brooder's furnace used to hover ;
When some got lost and from the rest would stray,
She'd take them in her big red hands and hold
Them to her breast till warm and calm they lay.
At last she'd put them back beneath the cover.

MISS MAYBEE

She and her mother lived, safe-housed in stone,
On interest from her father's bonds, but when
Her mother died of stomach cancer, then
Miss Maybee lived on interest all alone.
The shingles of Miss Maybee's house grew roan-
Streaked grey to match the shingles of her hair ;
Her face was like a flower, unsoiled by wear
Of children's fingers, but its bloom had gone.

One night a bunch of drunks upon a spree
Rang her door-bell. One kissed her, said, 'Baby,
I want your love.' Her face was flushed and red,
And all her body trembled like a tree:
'I cannot give you what you want,' she said,
'But God be thanked for what you've asked of me.'

GEORGE ERNST

George Ernst went in for horses all his life.
Though he was poor, no matter how things went
He kept the best team in the settlement,
Bit-keen and mated for the hauler's strife.
He'd never let a blacksmith use a knife
But pared their hoofs as if those hoofs were gold;
They ate more oats and hay than what he sold.
Men said he loved them better than his wife.

He paid nine hundred dollars' interest
Upon a thousand dollar loan; then pressed,
He had to sell his team to save his lands.
While dealers dickered and the sheriff sold,
He stood and gripped their bridles in his hands.
I never saw a man who looked so old.

GEORGE BURROUGHS

Although George Burroughs often used a knife,
As farmers must, to castrate or to kill,
He took no pleasure in the touch of steel.
As one who loved to feel things come to life
Beneath his hands, to end the patient strife
Of calving heifers pleased him best of all.
He liked the springtime better than the fall,
But all his farm was fruitful save his wife.

They say that when the doctor came last Spring
And said that he could never have a child,
Although he neither stormed nor acted wild,
He would not let the seed-drill work his lands
But walked the barren fields himself, sowing
The seed broadcast with quick jerks of his hands.

FRANK KIRKMICHAEL

There always was a crazy streak that ran
Right through the whole Kirkmichael family;
They all died off till only Patrick, Lee,
Young Dan, and Frank remained of all the clan.
They farmed for years together till young Dan
Jumped in the deep pool that he used to fish in;
Pat cut his throat next in the farmhouse kitchen,
And Lee went to the Asylum in a van.

Then Frank all by himself lived there and died.
He was not queer at all, but not a neighbour
Went near his place. All day outdoors he'd labour;
In Summer, Spring, and Fall, he'd sleep outside;
Long Winter nights he'd carve sap-spiles alone,
Hearing the wind like spirit voices moan.

SAM STOVER

When his day's work was done, Sam hardly ever
Did anything but whittle like a fool.
He'd sit there, making not some useful tool
Like an axe-handle, but queer things you'd never
See the like of, though some folks thought them clever.
He never liked my watching while he worked,
And how he acted once when he was irked
Comes back to me as clear today as ever.

'What are you whittling, Sam?' 'A girl,' he said.
I looked at it: 'A girl? But where is she?'
'I have her here all right,' he tapped his head,
'But she won't go into the wood for me.'
'Why don't you take her picture, work from that?'
He looked and looked at me, and then he spat.

ART

On dance-hall nights, or after sermon-tide
When youthful blood was warmed by talk of sin,
The curly-headed hellion with the grin
Would pick a girl and take her for a ride.
Hardly a miss along the river side
Escaped the price he always asked for carriage;
From him girls learned the basic fact of marriage
Although he made no one of them his bride.

Now Art is bald; a gold tooth spoils his style;
Here in the Farmer's Store he clerks inside,
Where buxom farmers' wives with matron-pride
Show him their half-grown children. At his smile
They grope with memories, grown vague and dim,
To wonder what they ever saw in him.

SAM WHITE

I hear Sam White, the hired man, is dead —
He used to work the farm for Michael Power
And tell us dirty stories by the hour
While we would listen in delight and dread.
The beat of him I've never heard nor read:
He could so well the facts of life express
We swallowed all his yarns and did not guess
That all the sex he knew was in his head.

But more than deacon or than parson yet
We felt his influence in the neighbourhood,
And little boys, attempting to be good,
When they'd 'come out' in meeting, down would get
Upon their knees and pray they might forget
What Sam White told them — but they never could.

DEACON JOHNSON

Old Deacon Johnson gave no groundhog board
Upon his farm; he'd root them out with water,
Earth up their holes, and set dogs to the slaughter,
Though he was kindly in both act and word.
It seemed each spring a flood of rodents poured
Upon his land to sink their shafts in clay,
But no one laughed in meeting when he'd pray,
'No more torment me with thy groundhogs, Lord.'

For all of us assembled understood
The Deacon's hate of groundhogs and his dread
Remembering how, beside the Monquart Wood,
Aiming where fog and forest overlap,
He lightly thought to shoot a groundhog's head
And put a bullet through his brother's cap.

HAL TOMS

Hal could not bear to hear the frantic squealing
Of hogs before they felt the butcher-knife;
He'd flinch to watch a field-mouse lose its life
When through the beater's teeth we'd chuck it reeling.
His father called him chicken-hearted for his feeling
And said: 'The boys who only stand and watch
The rest at swimming don't amount to much;
Next time we kill, you, Hal, will do the killing.'

With knife gripped hard and trembling tense he stood,
While two men held it rigid on its back;
He did not hear the squeals that used to rack
Nis nerves, so rapt he was. His stab was fast,
The stuck hog died, as spurts of crimson blood
Sprinkled his hands. He was a man at last.

ALOYSIUS SULLIVAN

Each Sunday morning if the day was clear
Before St. Vincent's steps we'd get together
And talk about our crops and wonder whether
Potatoes would be cheap again this year.
Then boys from far would meet with girls from near
As mothers smiled and ceased to watch for danger
Because they knew quite well each handsome stranger
Could hardly be a Protestant, and here.

But when the Father came, into the pale
Strained light we'd step, and not a single noise
Except the Latin and the bell would come.
One by one we'd go before the altar rail
Like strangers in a lonely land, come home
To the one place where union needs no voice.

NEW BRUNSWICK

Before it takes the air in greener shoots
A seed is nurtured by surrounding soil
And patterned by whatever streams can coil
Where worms and borers worked their slow pursuits;
And though it wills to grow a crown that fruits
In skies where lightnings break and thunders clap,
It can't escape the source that feeds its sap:
No tree belies its soil, outgrows its rootss.

Not soft the soil where we took root together;
It grew not giants but the stunted strong,
Toughened by suns and bleak wintry weather
To grow up slow and to endure for long;
We have not gained to any breadth or length,
And all our beauty is our stubborn strength.

DEATH WATCH

No thought or act of mine can twist
The fate that ticks upon my wrist;
Its sixty seconds deeper prod
My body's stake towards the sod,
And every pause becomes to me
An ominous eternity,
And should I tear the watch apart
Each tick would echo in my heart.

Its stubborn seconds drag me to
A last reluctant *rendez-vous*
Where one I do not wish to know
Waits still in time's black bagnio;
There she will hold me on her bed
Until my lust of life is dead
And all the urge to find release
Has poured itself to final peace.

But though I feel death's arms enfold
To rob me of my living gold,
The wench has gifts to recompense
The last surrender of my sense;
Unlike those wrung from human love
Her charms I cannot weary of:
Long worms destroy alike remorse
And longing for a second course.

TWO FEARS

the fear of death
is a cold clean breath
that the lungs reject

but a fungus rife
that few suspect
is the fear of life

in draught-proof walls
we put our trust
and die of rust

THE SEED I SOWED, BELIEVING

The seed I sowed, believing
In an everlasting rose,
Is now a stalk, unleaving
Its harvest to the snows,
And from its green-leafed fire
There's only left to burn
The stiff bone of the briar,
The cold-glossed hollow thorn.

Though bitter sap is squeezing
Where once a sweet glow ran,
My twisted stalk is seizing
These comforts while it can:
Although no bud shall splinter
Fresh leaves to greet the spring,
The briar will last out winter,
The thorn be sharp to sting.

WINTER APPLES

As winter apples stored in bins
A fragrant heat keep on
And sweeten in their wrinkled skins
Though suns of seasons gone,

The loves I stole from summer's tree
And plucked before their prime
In winter bins of memory
Grow sweeter all the time.

LOST COINCIDENCE

My lust and love revolve
around the orbit of the brain
as moving points oppose
each other round a circle's plane;

always they touch and pass
to arcs of shame and penitence
where each endures alone
the pain of lost coincidence.

BIGOT

In his mind's forest
a sapling bright
one-sidedly
grew to the light

till towering high
firm-rooted it stood
and blocked the sun
from the rest of the wood.

BUTTERFLY

Bedraggled now and crushed,
frail soul of fluttering things,
forgive my hands that brushed
the sun dust from your wings;

for though I turn and twist
in weak attempts to flee,
hard hands I can't resist
shall do the same to me.

DIALECTIC OF BIRTH

O hands and feet and heart and head,
Too tight the space that loved us curled,
And so we beat our stubborn way
From womb into the outer world,

Only to find that greater womb
In which our atom lives are stored,
Where many feed us in one's stead
Through our own age's navel cord;

But still we feel the space that binds
Is yet for us too strait a tie
And bruise ourselves against the walls
And wound the house of life thereby,

Until the world that holds us shakes
And through its pain draws freer breath
When we have burst this womb of life
Into the greater birth of death.

DIALECTIC

No moe on altars round
The sacred goats are bled;
No corybantics bound
With whips of sanguine red;
The gore-crows, hunger-led
Desert their holy ground;
The old cruel gods are dead,
The gentle Christ is crowned.

No more God's faithful hound
In search of souls is sped;
Each sin at which He frowned
Is a complex now instead:
The unrepentant dead
Sleep quiet in the ground;
The master Christ is fled,
The Freudian man is crowned.

No more the ego's ground
Encroaches on the id;
No Oedipus is found
By his fixation fed;
No paranoic dread
Grips nations in its round;
The Freudian man is dead,
The Atom God is crowned.

THE TWO THIEVES

When he had done his worst
All Joy from me to part
Death left one treasure still
To keep alive my heart;

But as I hugged it to me
Came Time, a subtler thief,
And softly stole away
Death's heritage of Grief.

A BALLAD OF LOVING

We stripped our bodies naked
When we were lass and lad,
And still I've not forgotten
The white, clean flesh we had.

And had we gone no further
We both had stayed content,
For flesh to flesh in nature
Is fair and innocent.

But our rash, youthful loving,
Its flesh-look satisfied,
Then stripped our souls as naked
To feed our mutual pride.

And love died out in horror
That flesh could not control —
God's love alone, I'm thinking,
Should see a naked soul!

INCIDENT

on the grey edge
of consciousness
where vast tides press
the mind's thin ledge

through blue waves of sleep
she swam to me,
Aphrodite
unbound from the deep.

she stabbed at me
without a word
with the white cold sword
of her beauty.

desperate I fled
that hungry strand
to a teacup land
of butter and bread

where maids are free
of dangerous wish
and only fish
rise from the sea,

but the terrible steel
left wounds of fear
on eye, tongue and ear
that will not heal.

BROOK REVISITED

There where the brook
shallows to run,
under the fading sun
I paused to look

at the amber flow,
and over the stones
rippled the same low tones
heard years ago,

and there at last
the trout I took
cool from the friendly brook
of my boy's past

had revenge on me,
hooked like a fish
by cruel barbs of wish
and memory.

AN INVOCATION

She is your priestess
And for you doth dress
Her glowing flesh to shine
Like sacrificial wine,

And I am your priest,
Offering as feast
My pure unleavened bread
Of goodly manlihead;

Bear we your ritual
Without words at all —
A service catholic
Where sound is heretic —

Now the moon at night
Makes your altar bright,
And for your savour blows
The incense of the rose;

Now sweet wine and bread
On the grass lie spread
As tabled in a room,
Come, Love, your feast consume.

A BALLAD OF ORCHARD EVENING

Out in an orchard evening
They walked without a word,
And apple buds in moonlight
Above them swelled and stirred.

Out in an orchard evening
They walked through apple bowers
And on them fell the honey
Of gently swaying flowers.

Now back from orchard evening
They come without a word,
But deadly hangs the silence
Between them like a sword,

And lips that kiss at parting
Are now a hail-hard shower
To bruise and shred and mangle
The fragments of a flower.

THE BUTTERFLY

Young Ben with net and jar would run a mile
To catch a brand-new butterfly to add
To his collection; neighbours thought him mad —
Hobbies like his are not New Brunswick's style.

One day when Ben came back from useless chase
His feeble-minded aunt who'd watched him run
Gave him, bursting with pride for what she'd done,
A bag of crumpled paper tied with lace.

Impatiently he tore away the string
And found a common Cabbage Butterfly
Too spent to move a rubbed and tattered wing.
He crushed it in his hand in quick disdain.
Too late he saw a wingéd thing in pain
Die in the round jar of her clouded eye.

THE BALLAD OF JOHN ARMSTRONG

John Armstrong was a navvy
Whom twisting winds had hurled
To stoke the black tramp-steamers
On the seven seas of the world.

He sat with his friends at poker.
His gambling luck was the worst.
He turned up the Queen of Hearts,
Threw down the cards and cursed.

He walked out on the aft-deck
Above the engine jars,
He leaned his hand on the rail
And he looked at the stars.

John Armstrong leaned on the rail
And wondered where was joy,
But the moon blinked down from the sky,
It doesn't matter, boy.

They anchored in the Tiber,
The crew-boat shoreward hove,
And with it went John Armstrong
To find a sailor's love.

She sat and drank his cocktails
In a cabaret in Rome,
Her black eyes said, *Come hither,*
But her red mouth said, *Go home.*

He walked the crowded alleys
After they closed the bars.
He put his hand on a lamppost
And he looked at the stars.

John Armstrong leaned on a lamppost,
What he wanted didn't come,
But the moon blinked down from the sky,
It doesn't matter, chum.

The next port was Marseilles:
Though swift the sailors throng,
When they came to the French bordel
The first was John Armstrong.

She took the francs he gave her.
She paid what she did owe,
Kissed him a skilful kiss
And said, *Va-t-en, matelot.*

He walked out in the moonlight
And the city streets were dark,
But the lonely hawk within him
Was singing like a lark.

John Armstrong leaned on a lamppost
Full of the joy he had,
But the moon blinked down from the sky,
It doesn't matter, lad.

The ship put in to Plymouth
Where his boy's life was led.
In the church of St. David
He and Sal were wed.

John Armstrong walked in the garden
In the cool of the night;
He left his wife fast sleeping
Lost in her love's delight.

John Armstrong leaned on his own gate,
Said, *This is journey's end.*
But the moon blinked down from the sky,
It doesn't matter, friend.

THE DRAGON TREE

Strange-scented birds and song-flowers grow
In the garden where I cannot go,
Where green-trunked trees grey apples hold
And blue fish swim in pools of gold.

And always there a green sun glows
To burn the song of the red-leafed rose,
While yellow grasses bend their knees
Before a bluebird-smelling breeze.

Around the garden's circle flies
The dragon-tree to eat the skies
With silver-scented fruit that sings
Hid in the branches of its wings.

That garden now to me is gone
Where sight and sound and sense are one,
But children walk there still before
They eat the dragon's cherished store.

WAVE-CHILL

Shivered out of wave-chill, glimmering
water, boy-naked to a naked fear,
he water fresh, salt, oil-dulled, shimmering,
could never after waking bear

whose sleep is sure and swift with slipping
dreams through currents cold and clear
to where sleek sirens sing, salt water dripping
moon-pearls from their gleaming hair.

THE GOLDEN FISH

The golden fish beneath the stones
That line the bottom of the lake
Will never rise to greet my will
Although I stir the surface up
With hollow reeds of sight and sound;
But when I drown myself in sleep
They dart alive and ripple through
The shining waters of my dreams.

SUCCUBA

. . . silver-limbed in the room's night
and the thick air
she swam to me through moonlight
as empty and as fair,

and a blood-pulse beating within
quickened and rushed
through the dove's wing of her skin
wherever mine it brushed ...

now my ghost (knowing other ways
by which men fell)
thanks the devil all its days
for the sweetest road to hell.

THE JACKS OF HISTORY

"This is the house that Jack built"

The house in which grandfather lived
was fashioned like a spire;
so high it was that heaven seemed
only a little higher.

Before he reached sufficient height
to touch the topmost spot
his bulging sides burst through the walls
and shattered all the lot.

My father's house was like a bank
of broad and ample girth,
with pillared beams and low flat roof,
a house that loved the earth.

Before he filled its gross extent
his head the roof did rap
till headaches made him take it off
to free his thinking cap.

Now naked in a growing storm
without a house at all
I run from grandpa's wall-less roof
to father's roofless wall.

THE IDIOT ANGEL

God has given a playground of moving toys
Set in a garden of trees and flowers
To an idiot angel to play in forever.

Silent on swift feet — anywhere, everywhere —
Constantly clutching at movement and colour
Or jostling the toys together with a laugh of thunder
Moves the delighted angel.

At his touch, all flowers lose their colour;
With his breath, all toys lose their motion.
The toys have a name for him.
Although they cannot see where he is
They see his work in the garden . . .
Of late he seems to be quicker and stronger.

DESCENT FROM EDEN

That year the rich banana harvest failed,
When infants tore their mother's milkless dugs
And tasted blood and whined, the wisest apes
Forsook the shelter of the friendly trees,
Leaving their virtue on the leafy limbs.

Stark hunger snapped the tree-forged gentleness
That shuddered at the acrid smell of blood;
The clammy horror of the crawling caves
Fished back the feral lust to feed on flesh
From cold, ancestral seas that knew no sun
Until, sharking in schools again their prey
Through tangled bottoms of a greener sea,
They grew the scourge and terror of the earth.

But still the tree-shaped hands of infants clung
About their mothers' necks, prolonging thus,
Like cords umbilical, the natal ties;
And sometimes when the birds of morning sang
A tree would grow inside an apish head
With fruit and innocence among its boughs,
And there the ape would from his fellows climb
To drink the golden waters of the sun
Before returning to his night of blood.

OUR SMALL-TOWN LOVES

O golden-barged above the gleaming Nile
Or splendid in the halls of marble Troy,
Illicit lovers flaunted lawless joy
And triumphed by magnificence of style.

And, later, Lancelot and Guinevere,
The wise monk, Abelard, and Heloise,
In stony cells upon their bleeding knees
For long years proved their guilty loves sincere.

Of these the poets sang. They cannot sing
Our small-town loves. Let tabloid prose present
Cheap hotel bedrooms where a door-bell's ring
Strips off the condom sheer of sentiment.
We sheathe no seeds of grandeur nor of prayer
But only flesh and swollen fear's despair.

JOHN

John came to high school from a country farm,
A string-bean with a stammer in his speech
And eyes that always moved beyond your reach
To hide the shy conceit that meant no harm.

Its social life was half of high school's charm,
But not for John. He stayed at home and read
Sir Walter Scott and Tennyson instead
Of keeping some bright dance-hall partner warm.

A new girl came to class, and John was caught
Although he did not speak to her; in short,
He loved her in the best book-loving way,
Fought down bad thoughts, and swore he would be true,
Nor knew her as the other fellows knew:
A common bit who gave herself away.

THE RETURN

When Ben came back to town again, he said:
"What matter if the girl did love you when
 You jilted her; both time and other men
 Can close the wounds you made; no doubt she's wed."

When Ben came back to town again, he said
"That young first love we took so much to heart
 I've most forgot; and she, at least in part,
 Has too; and when we meet we'll know it's dead."

Still proud and tall she walked the common ground
To meet him there. He searched her face unmarred
By lines, and in her no-more-wincing eyes
He saw the little whips of love that wound
The heart within and leave the skin unscarred
Were dead . . . He wished the things he'd said were lies.

BETH

The ignorance in which her youth was buried
Was early lost among the dance-hall sport
Her set took part in, but young Beth got caught,
Made pregnant by a man already married.
Then all the saints and uncaught sinners queried
The gait and growing girth of that poor gaby;
They tittered, whispered, "Beth will have a baby."
And only stopped when Beth at last miscarried.

I wonder if the angleworms that glut
Their hunger on our human bones' rich lime
Will strike from it a slimier sort of worming
And slither round the pool at fishing time
To watch a luckless sister's frantic squirming
As some one shoves a fish-hook up her gut.

THE WIDOWER

Not lonely now in bed the widower lies
Who late at night has felt the smooth-skinned swell
Of rounded sheets arouse his skin to flame
Or in his dreams, like Ixion in hell,
Has clasped a curve of softness that became
A cloudy pillow to his morning eyes.
Such nightmare waking not tonight applies;
It is warm flesh that meets his warmer thighs.

Warm flesh and tendered in such tender wise
He feels his love return and all the black
Life-loneliness lie conquered on its back
There in the dark one passion-breathing space
Before his mind recalls the raddled face
Of his love-machine and her hard, glazed eyes.

THE ROCK PILE

Right in the middle of a field there stands
A huge rockpile, but most of it is one
Big stone, a lump of rock that weighs a ton
Or more, too much for horses or for hands
To budge, and there the man who cleared those lands,
Jim Armstrong, in the days of brawn and grit,
Wrestled for weeks in vain to lever it;
It broke his harness, traces, grappling bands.

And so Jim covered up with little stones
The only thing in life he could not beat;
But when new settlers came after a while
To look and praise in awed, admiring tones
The mighty rockpile in his field, he'd smile
A twisted smile and find the credit sweet.

JACK

When all the pails upon the stove were spilling
The men would take them to the scalding trough;
There Jack would watch the water swirl like broth
On wood still bristled from the last year's killing.

But though the lad was keen and more than willing,
His father thought him young for such a matter;
He with his dog was banished from the slaughter;
They only got the sound of frantic squealing.

But in the kitchen by themselves, the boy
Would clutch the leaping terrier on the floor;
Then both would crouch before the kitchen door
And tremble with a wild and eager joy
Which came and went in waves on every cry
That swept across the distance from the sty.

NO MAN CAN TRUST HIS FAIREST LOVE IS KIND

No man can trust his fairest love is kind,
For art has alchemy so subtly bold
It turns base metal into seeming gold;
And faith in Nature's goodness is as blind.
For under ripeness of the apple's rind
Corruption often soils exploring teeth,
And sour whey may lurk in depths beneath
The cream of goodness in a placid mind.

Since this is so, I shall not risk a test
And lose you quite. Indeed there is no need.
Still on your beauty shall my senses feed,
While from the best ingredients of dessert
In me I shall create blood, soul, and heart,
An inner you, as perfect as the rest.

FOR GOOD FRIDAY

The body writhing on contorted hips
Hung hard and magnified the crimson star
Upon each palm; blood mixed with vinegar
Stung sharp the nerves along the broken lips;
The bruised ribs throbbing from the corded whips
Had not subsided in the welted side,
And yet the spirit kept its loving pride
Untouched above the animal's eclipse.

Within that spirit's centre crystalline
Reality was changed from gross to fine:
There hate-pocked faces wavered, broke, and blurred
Like sea-flowers seen through wind-driven seas;
And there the hiss of every venomed word
Dwindled to wind and waved the olive trees.

THE CROSS-GRAINED TREE

With axe and adze slow Joseph hewed the tree
And scowled to watch the way its cross-grain curled,
Nor dreamed such poor and knotty wood would be
A lathe on which his son would turn the world.

THE DANCERS

Though of infinity we dancers own
Brief floors of space, thin walls of time, and dance
A spot dance halted by the caller, Chance,
The music's sweet; we do not dance alone.

TURN ABOUT

That *turn about* is fair I won't agree
Now time I used to waste is wasting me.

AN IRONY

Though time's sure touch has now erased
The lines that grief so sharply traced,
Her epitaph engraved in stone
Lives on to mock his feeling gone.

THE WATCH

In vain I backwards turn and twist
The wrist-watch hands upon my wrist
Which every time I turn remind
Me of a watch I can't rewind.

ELECTION SPEECH

My words beat at the walls of thought's chamber
Like wild wings in a lethal jar,
Butterfly-weighted against the invisible
Cold barrier of things as they are.

The glass-mould of a lifetime leaves no fissure
For reason or rhetoric to dent —
Heart-high around them suffuses
Cyanide vapour of self-content.

PHILANDER

Narcotic love (a cigarette
Which, burning, deadens its own fire)
Discards all memory of a smoking past
With the butt-ending of desire.

But anywhere at any time
Each new combustible when met
Will scratch again the matchbox heart
To light another cigarette.

ELEGY FOR A BAD PAINTER

Pour his blood into scarlet tubes
and drill a palette from his hollow skull
pluck soft brushes out of his blonde hair
and on the greybone easel of his limbs
stretch out the canvas of his flayed skin

he who could not make a picture living
should have the chance to make one now. . . .

THE WOMAN

OVER and over, in company or alone,
This woman talks of her trouble.
At night, in love with the misery
Of tortured nerve-ends, her mind
(Like a child's fingernail squeezing
Fresh pus from an old wound)
Tears off all the work-day has healed.
And the sore spreads.

HER PURITY

Her purity was like the snow
That dazzles back a distant sun
And chills the hand of flesh that dares
To violate so white a one;

Her purity was like the snow
Whose frost no pressure long withstands—
I never knew the dirt it hid
Until it melted in my hands.

TO A COQUETTE

Now you at last have crucified
My love upon your cross of pride
Don't hang around the grave, my dear;
There'll be no resurrection here.

A CHRISTMAS PETITION

To see men use God's holy things
To swell the merchant's hoard
Awoke your wrath in temple once
To swing a knotted cord;
Your eyes were lit with lightnings then,
Your tongue a sharp-edged sword—
Pray come not back at Christmas now,
Jesus Christ, my Lord.

ODE TO FREDERICTON

White are your housetops, white too your vaulted elms
That make your stately streets long aisles of prayer,
And white your thirteen spires that point your God
Who reigns afar in pure and whiter air,
And white the dome of your democracy—
The snow has pitied you and made you fair,
O snow-washed city of cold, white Christians,
So white you will not cut a black man's hair.

THE FOOL

Though in my ear a hundred dogmas shout,
I do not know the gods divine
Who light for me the lamps that shine
In women's faces, food, and wine:
I only know the fool who puts them out.

A POEM

When thoughts are springs tight-wound in space
And geared to words that mesh in place
A poem is a watch designed
To tick forever in the mind.

CONVENTION

I could not tear down the walls that hemmed me in.
For every stone I dropped a hundred hands
Sprang up to put it back in place again.

At last I asked those willing workers:
"Know you not that when these walls are razed
You will be free?"   "This place is safe," they said,
"Against the rocs and unicorns outside."

THE TOP OF KEIRSTEAD MOUNTAIN

High on the top of Keirstead Mountain, morning cold
Under an eggshell sky, the rich-yoked sun
Pulses outward to fold me, shimmering
And warm in amoebic arms of gold;
And the smooth-skinned air, powdered with pollen,
Brushes me with kisses, moving over my flesh
More delicate-soft than those of a woman.

Here on the heap of this high hill—grateful
For the sky's shell-heaven, and the sun's arms,
The feathery, cool kiss of a fledgling wind—
I stand and know in what thin sense these charms
Are given: light love squandered as free
On the bare, air waste as on any life that breathes,
And clouded soon with storms as meaningless.

But here and high—atop of the moment morning
That gives all it has and asks me for nothing—
What meaning has meaning where feeling is all?
Why should I care on what ways will wander
These winds that wanton me now? Will it matter
Days when the brooding sun clutches hereafter
Others under the shell of an eyeless sky?

DIANA

All free and fair
above the skeins
of tangled air
she rides

with what sure laws
and invisible chains
she draws
the tides

deep in the blue
salt blood of the sea
even as you
draw me

IN THESE FALL WOODS

In these fall woods
when I was
a girl an old
man took me
down and made
me want
it scared

but he could
not do it and
he cried

I ran away
and never told

but here
in these fall woods
recalling how
gnarled hands
clutched earth

and remembering
the tearing sounds
shaking his frail
shoulders
I think of what
ma said
the day she threw
out the chipped and
leaky bowl, no
longer beautiful,

and wonder if he
had poured out
his weak sad
desire that day
would it seem
here now different
in these fall woods
spent among withered leaves.

THE WATER AND THE ROCK

Hard rock was I, and she was water flowing,
Over sharp stones of opposition going;
Shaping herself to me as to a cup,

She filled the valleys of my ego up
With a cool, smooth compliance, everywhere
As yielding and unhurtable as air.

Soft was my love as water, and I forgot
In the calm wash of complaint rhythm caught
How water shapes and softens, sculpts and smooths
The channel of the rock through which it moves.

DISPLACED

Not plants only but human seed
Put forth blind arms to fill a need:
Horizontal roots that twine and coil
Reach outward through the social soil:
Safe through the years, their foothold good,
Ours grow upon familiar food.

By cruel winds of force and fear
Uprooted from their atmosphere
Our brothers come. Their maimed arms grope
Through alien soil for food and hope
To find where soft and rich we fare
A rocky hardness everywhere.

THE FIELD OF FLESH

The will's steel ploughshare turns, and gilt
Frail weeds of hot, spent summer fall.

Blanketed by frozen fear, they rot
In nerves that underlie the cold.

What crops will rise to batten on
The humus of this slow decay

When frost is thawed by purring winds
And passion seeds the flesh again?

HAWK AND HERON

Oh wild and hungry
Grew the hawk in me.

I slipped the leash
And let it flesh,

But its rage had chilled
And hunger stilled

Back softly it swept
To my mind and slept.

Now without a hood
It cries for blood. . . .

A SUNBEAM ROLLED THE STONE AWAY

A sunbeam rolled the stone away
From off the grave of murdered love,
And from these walls of bone and clay
There rose by miracle a dove.

It gave a little joyous cry
And flew, all light and free from pain:
Nor can I coax, for all I try
It back to death with me again.

WHEN THE SWITCH THAT TIME CORRODES

When the switch that time corrodes
clicks hard against the will
and a flash-back bulb explodes
a long-forgotten cell,

flesh that died two decades back
reactivates its pain;
in the room my mind kept black
light breaks the heart again

to show through gathering dust
that thick on the image lies
the face of my ruined lust,
the hell in her tortured eyes.

LEFTY

I wonder what's become of Lefty
who lived with the old people next door
and pitched for our high school
back home when I was a boy.
(Folks said he was their daughter's son,
a burlesque queen in the city,
and they smacked their lips, remembering . . .)

He was loose-armed and very fast
and couldn't throw a straight ball.
No use using signals,
he was too wild for that.
So when I caught him
with that beat-up catcher's mitt
he broke three fingers.
I guess I was lucky.
Boys who put boxing gloves
on with him got worse,
Lefty loved hurting things,
breaking them up.

He was handsome and smart,
but few of us liked him,
he was self-independent,
all coiled up in himself
like a broody hen.
I called him that once
and he turned dead white:

"Don't Fred, don't call me that.
A hen is a barnyard whore.
Why, she'll squat right down
and let the roosters ride her

in the dirt anywhere.
There's nothing in the world
I hate like a hen."
So I let him alone.

He liked me, I suppose,
as much as he could like any one.
He used to lend me books about baseball.
I remember the day I brought one back.
All his folks were away
And Lefty was out in the shed
whistling, *"I wish I had a girl*
like the girl who married dear old dad."
I guess I should have knocked
but I didn't.
I opened the door and walked right in.

There was Lefty and there was the hen.
He had her hung up with a cord
round her neck too tight for a squawk,
and he was sawing off her legs
with a dull jacknife. Sawing and whistling . . .

He heard me as I walked in
and turned, standing there,
and you could almost have heard
the blood dripping from the end
of the knife-blade for a moment.
"You son of a whore," I said.
"You son of a whore."
And Lefty broke and cried like a girl,
And I left.

That night he ran away
and I never saw him again.

I wonder where Lefty is now.
Wherever he is, I know
he is still hurting,
breaking faces, hearts maybe,

hitting at a world
he couldn't forgive for making
him a son of a whore.

THE ECONOMIST BURNS

The economist burns
With my response.   I do not tell
Him the law of diminishing returns
Is time's as well

He loves, and I content
Reciprocate his active throes
(Our passion pays an evening's rent
That boredom owes);

But twenty years ago
A beat-up doll thrust in my arms
Could make my body burn and glow
More than his charms.

SNAKE SHADOW

Light breaks in me
and jungle shrinks
to snake shadow

under light's skin
still and stealthy
shadow gnaws

swollen and cruel
with the blood of light
it grows

who dares to let it out?
who can hold it in?

THEIR HANDS AND OURS . . .

Their hands and ours
ape-clenched now hold
not flowers but guns'
lead arguments
whose brimstone smell
is death to right
and wrong, but theirs
are evil, ours good . . .

and this men swear
for truth who would
not dare to say
when two limbs rub
on a sick tree
in a black wind:
"These must have come
from different seed."

A CHRISTMAS CAROL

The holly wreath that now
Our house adorns
Will wither soon and be
A jagged crown of thorns;

Nor when fir needles fall
Can tinsel hide
The grey and naked limbs
Of the tree crucified;

The fair feast of Christmas
Our flesh enthrones
Even as we gaze piles up
A hollow heap of bones;

By which I know a sad
And doleful thing
That though we eat and drink
And gladsome carols sing

The ancient curse still blights
The human tree
And things men touch become
Shadows of Calvary.

THE WEB: FOR EASTER

Our feet that danced on morning ways
slowed to a fumbling crawl
as one by one the outward rays
broke on a narrowing wall;

then as we searched beneath the eaves
of slanting light and cloud,
the web the greedy spinner weaves
closed round us like a shroud;

and when One came Who laughed at loss
and braved its inmost lair
where taut threads joined to form a cross,
the spider caught Him there;

but as in blood our hope decayed
out of His seeded heart
He, dying, grew a thin green blade
that thrust the web apart.

THE WINTER OF THE TREE

The leaf has vanished and the bud.
No soil now feeds the root's bare skin.
The tree must live inside the tree
On hoarded sap—starved, roving blood
That hunts more bitter and more thin
Through trunk and limbs where no buds bring
A latent hope that flowing spring
May leaf in green futurity.

Locked in its core of memory
Under a gathered skin of snow
The sap of passion-burning sun
Still stirs—a salt, seed-carrying sea
That moves and finds no place to go;
Twisting through arteries that lead
Nowhere, the living waters bleed
And vanish one by one.

Now powerless to alter fate
And stirred by ancient memory
To undertake creative acts
That lack both sun and soil to mate,
In this last winter of the tree
How shall the cells that still draw breath
Caught in the body of its death
Resist the borer or the axe?

WITHIN MY TEMPLED FLESH

Within my templed flesh
a god of pain presides
over love's slow murders
and hate's long suicides.

I curse him as I feel
his unrelenting sway
but could a force less cruel
wring living out of clay?

LOST DIMENSION

I from my myness
must a you create
for your yourness
is inviolate.

Likewise your yourness
makes the me you have known,
for my myness
is all my own

Hard spheres are we
whose edges join,
seeking to grasp
an illusion,

that lost dimension
whose laws are such
not circumference
but centres touch.

THE GRAFTING

In place of limb from me lopped off
by sharp desire's shining knife
I thrust a scion of his life
and shielded it by wax of love
against the spores of rot that lie
habitual in society.

Filled by one sap, fed from one root,
the grafting took, and part of him
became a part of me, a limb
fast-joined to bear its sweeter fruit
and justify what both must share,
the mutilation and the scar.

LYCANTHROPY

O wolf of Love, whose green eyes gleam
Through darker thickets of my dream,
Though me you bit and slew beside
Sweet Chastity, my lamb of pride,
And flayed it of the woolly white
That hid the flesh of my delight,
I did not mind its death the least,
But howled with you and joined the feast.

BLACK WIDOW

She wound him round with thread
that choked the will to move
and fed till he was bled
of all red-blooded love;

now gentled by her use
he loves his fate so much
he only dreads to lose
that paralysing touch,

accepting as fair play
her role and his, the more
for having marked her, prey;
himself, the predator.

AFTER

With the sun's kiss to warm
My body there,
And the wind's cool charm
To finger my hair,

Still shall I lie,
And covet no lass—
Sky-loved . . . when I
Am sand and grass.

A PHANTOM I

To a gap in the trees
where tall canes grow
red raspberries
I go once more
and I eat
ripe fruit again
and its sour-sweet
taste like pain
touches a tender sore.

For things are real
and cannot die;
men are the ghosts that feel . . .
Drowned in the cruel
mill-race
of time's stream
a phantom I
haunts the old place
for an old dream.

THE HALOED TREE

Night and day join
in a life dance
thin balanced on
an edged ignorance

as innocent buds
tremble and swell
with sap that floods
upward from hell

and root bestiality
gropes through its lair
that the haloed tree
may bloom and be fair.

BIG CYRUS

Big Cyrus in the old religion trod.
He was no reed whom winds of pleasure bowed;
With face as stony as the land he plowed
He read his Bible and he loved his God.

Scanning the heaven's face for frown or nod,
He watched his Master like a beaten dog,
But not a glimmer pierced the aweful fog
To show the clear intent—reward or rod.

And then he met a girl and thought the sign
That showed him numbered with the saints divine
Was in her love, but that was clothed in flesh
And flesh he knew was sin; caught in the mesh
Of indecision still he lingered on
Nor made his mind up till his chance was gone.

THE MAN WHO CLIMBED

"There'll be nothing at the end,"
They said, "Why go on?"

They watched him toil, a dizzy speck
Against the dread and secret mountain
Where no one else had been,
And all their lives thereafter
Were stabbed with shame and secret doubts . . .

He stood alone on the empty peak
Underneath the mocking stars
And knew at last how right they were.

TAME GOOSE

Down high ways of heaven wild geese fly
the tame goose answers with a cry

along a ring of palings high
she stretches neck and runs to try
the mocking wings she can't control

but when the goose-girl brings the rye
she snatches up and gobbles whole
the grain safe nestling in the bowl

nor heeds the whistling wings gone by.

THE CROSS OF CONFORMITY

Not alone at Calvary
Was passion-tide,
A crucifixion
And a God who died;

For still the Pharisees
Of iron lands
To their iron cross
Bind the children's hands

Until they crucify
The gods in them
On twisted arms
Of pride and shame . . .

Not one but all must share
Rusty agonies
Which bring no Easter
When the spirit dies.

THE MYRIAD GHOSTS

The myriad ghosts of selves I've killed
That this one self might live instead
Come back through corridors long sealed
To throng around my bed.

I'd stand cold chill of hate's nightmare
Or searing heat of envy's cries;
These only look . . . I cannot bear
The pity in their eyes.

BURDENS

When I was young and strong and straight
No burdens on my back were laid,
So proud I took on me the weight
Of all the wrongs I never made.

It forced my knees down to the ground
And bent my back with bowed despair,
But when I took it off I found
I could no longer lightly fare;

For even as I said farewell,
Leaving the world's woes on the world's shelf,
There grew upon me like a shell
The heavier burden of myself.

ULYSSES MINOR

He waxed both ears to drown the luring song
The sirens sang beside the lonely sea,
For strings of life must break that vibrate long
To such great ecstasy.

Now in his mind their seething sea-bells chime
And soft, insidious passions wake to stir
Cruel ghosts that lurk between the ticks of time
And mock their murderer.

SWEET HAY

Sour is the summer hay
In forbidden fields;
Only the winter day
Sweet harvest yields.

After his quaking
duel
with conscience
and the cruel
tense
breaking
of her heart
are over
lady and lover
winter apart
on clover
time-cured and sweet
to chew and remember
from the mind's bin—
holding the heat
of passion September
minus the sweat
of regret
and the thistle of sin.

WHAT IF?

What if this universe that now
So badly ordered seems
Is but the nightmare of a god
Who cannot rule his dreams?

THE OLD GAME

"Go in and out the windows,
Go in and out the windows,
Go in and out the windows,
As you have done before."

In and out the windows I danced with dusty lies
And stirred the motes that dimmed my true love's lovely eyes;
Behind each pain I saw there sweet waters ebbed to clear,
But with our pride we damned them, as we had done before.

"Go up and down the valley,
Go up and down the valley,
Go up and down the valley,
As you have done before."

Up and down the valley I longed with young desire
To scorch her body's meadow in a lust-consuming fire,
But when at passion's touch our bodies' flame would soar
We drew back fearful then as we had done before.

"Go kneel before your lover,
Go kneel before your lover,
Go kneel before your lover,
For the golden gates are closed."

I knelt before my true love and offered her a ring,
And when she took it from me all birds began to sing.
She let me share an Eden of sweet and thornless rose,
But she grew another garden and the golden gates were closed.

THE GARDEN DAY

The children play
nor seek the shade
in the garden day
that time has made

like butterflies
blind to their doom
their light joys rise
to the minutes' bloom

on wings as weak
and frail as breath
they hide-and-seek
in the mouth of death

while slowly in
grinding and dull
closes the grin
of a hungry skull

and over the wall
on the bright parade
long shadows fall
from a hidden spade.

SOIREE

in nimble grooves
around the social tree
like clockwork moves
the tame menagerie:

white dove . . . soft lamb . . .
each pair so sweet that few
would guess them sham
to hide from prying view

two beasts fear-thrust
deep in a bone-barred cage,
lean leopard lust
and cold lioness rage

THE MASK

my father's father's face
that my own father wore
I now put on to hide
the tender parts within

but even as their smile
cold stiffens on my face
I feel the callous mask
slow penetrate the skin

my slender nerves control,
and now I know at last
why sire and grandsire moved
like robots in their homes

and hugged the waning life
of days that shone before
their wounded feelings donned
the Nessus mask of pride.

MARATHON DANCERS

on muscles wearied by the beat,
paired or alone the dancers glide
in desperation lest a pause
bring exit and the night outside

they know the tune is in their mind,
that if they stop the dance will stop,
and that unless they breathe the world
will shrink to limp balloon and drop

but as they toil with frantic feet
to keep in time ere time departs,
the only room their senses know
is shattered by their bursting hearts

THE REED

a reed once glittered
cleanly cool, slim-proud and tall
queen of cloudless air

a reed once danced
courtier to my breath and
trembled when I blew

when my weight of need
fell on it, the reed made one
with hard, wounding earth

when I rose it rose
again, glittering cool in
after-tempest calm

but I had learned to trust
my hollow heart no more

RIDER

strong in my summer range and prime
over the five-bar gate
of my will's corral upward I climb
to the unridden horse of my hate.

guilt-sharp spurs and a nail-pierced bridle,
quick cruel tugs on the bit of its pain,
then the weight of my worth on the saddle
till the beast in it's tired and tame;

when it stands head down and shaking,
too bruised to resist me or move,
I shall place on the hot flesh quaking
the soft cool hand of my love.

THE MAN-WORM

up the white-rose
hill of snow
the man-worm goes

slowly he moves
in a one-way groove
beyond his will

where air turns thin
and powder dry
and the sun's gold
burns cold in the sky.

now the last
blood-burst
of his joy-pain
is past

he leaves no stain
on time's cold rose

MOOD-PIECE

Plucked by the sliding fingers of now,
Thin strings in time's harp-bow,
We vibrate and wear and go.

Though now and then our sounds may join
In a sweet, short unison,
All too soon the tune is gone . . . .

As though a player blind and bent
Fumbled with the instrument,
In senility content

If from the strings his fingers wrung
Faint notes of the full song sung
When harp and he were young.

58

THE GARDEN

I know a garden where
each plant is thorned with scars
in vain by zealous care
of God's mad gardeners

who hack with holy steel
and shape to Rose the weeds
of space and time but fail
from evil in the seeds;

quick devil-bees, a host,
engage the springtime bloom
till even Rose is crossed
with plants of rank perfume

I know a garden where
true Rose lies under loam:
God's madmen still work there
and bees eat honeycomb.

INCIDENT

When the hired girl's sister called by surprise
And sat in the kitchen there with us all
We stripped off her pride with our fingering eyes
For we knew she was with child that fall.

But she stayed sullen and still to the visit's end,
And we grew ashamed and sorry as hell,
And our tongues tried a little too hard to pretend
Not to know what our eyes knew a little too well.

'Let me walk home with you,' I offered to soften
Her leaving. She blushed, but her eyes met my own:
'A girl who's walked home with the boys too often
Had better get used to walking alone.'

THE LIGHT THAT ONCE

The light that once in prehistoric seas
Propelled the lancing sperm
Is poisoned by the cells' disease
To feed the wars of rose and worm.

Then do not wake to light the sleeping girl,
Nor rouse her sea-salt blood;
Still round her loins let fig-leaves curl,
Let angels guard her dreams from flood.

FUNERAL DIRECTION

Let her whose flesh was flame
Not rot, but burn,
Nor let the dross lie tame
Inside an urn.

May wind and sun and air
The ash assume
That living could not bear
A narrow room.

THE CHOICE

White and frail on the moonlight's bed
Her body trembled and her eyes were bright,
But I kissed her a boy's good-night
And hurried home through the prickly wood.

Free and pure of all flesh-thorn scars
Was the love that pulsed to my marching blood,
But the moon drew chill behind a hood
Of clouds that blotted out the stars.

AT THE TREE'S RUBBED FOOT

at the tree's rubbed foot
where fat swine grunt and guzzle
and let no grass grow

the plum's frail blossom
a girl's tear-wet handkerchief
white against the mud

HITCHHIKER

Your dusty anger cooled as my car dipped
down over the hill's crest,
and you forgot the memory of me
when your feet drew to rest;

in vain I held the accelerator
to the floor all day through —
hard asphalt miles could not obliterate
my memory of you,

old wayside woman with the lifted hand
that like destiny
twisted to fist and hammered on my heart
after I passed you by.

JANUARY MORNING

. . . the storm-ending gold
of wind-fall dawn . . . naked trees
ermine-clad in cold

WATCHING THESE TWO

watching these two
flies on a pane
that clearly view
through glass between

but cannot touch,
I think how we
whose bodies clutch
sense unity

in our flesh are blind
to the dark core
of inner mind
that love should share

there are no keys
can penetrate
to it save these —
blunt words that grate

and wound the thin
nerved otherness
the deeper in
their edges press

though probing thus
might reach the best
each one of us
will shirk the test

each one will keep
half-tied, half-free
postponing deep
possibility

to easy peace
and partial love
an unrelease
where habits move

and bodies give
with no bliss or hurt
to minds that live
in rooms apart

where the noise of home
no deeper lies
than casual hum
of these two flies.

IN THIS BALANCED HOUR

now the old owl night
still as a grey-winged ghost slips
through glimmering trees

and low in the east
on shimmering wings the new
day's gold falcon climbs . . .

in this balanced hour
earth gathers back her soul and
breathes it to the grass

THE PARADOX OF BLOOD

Bigots in vain, the lovers rack
Each other's hearts with words and break
Their flesh to fit each other's dreams;
Nor can their equal lusts provide
Humbling fires for mutual pride.

Yet in each other's martyrdom
Each burns for miracle to come
When dream and flesh as one will join —
That catholic moment incense-thick
To which all words are heretic.

Still bigoted they meanwhile bear
And give each other wounds of fear,
Blind to the paradox of blood
That all who rise to true love's faith
Must lie together first in death.

THE SCAPE-GOAT

I saw the roll
of frightened eyes
that merged into my own.
I trembled with
the tremors of his skin.

Then I saw his face
was black as sin
with scalloped jaws
and knobbly bumps of bone
where horns in time would grow.

'He is the devil,' then
I thought, 'and I
will axe his neck
and when he's dead
I will be pure and good.'

Thus justified, I put
a finger in his mouth
and as he stretched
across the block to suck,
I swung the axe and cut.

The cheated jaws
unclosed, the head
dropped from my hand,
and with it dropped
the burden of my sin.

But as I turned
all free and clean to go
I felt warm spurts and saw
the hand that held
the axe was red.

PAUL

Paul's dream was born when he was altar boy
At Mass. As Father Kevin said, *Gratias
Agamus Domino Deo Nostro,* and he
Clear-voiced replied, *Dignum et justum est,*
He saw himself in Father Kevin's place
Before the altar, holding in his own
Right hand the flesh of God.

                      And for this dream
He prayed each day and did his lessons well
And never told his fellows at the school,
His teachers or his parents — holding back
The big surprise till after graduation.

He told it first one April party night
In his last highschool year. The guests had gone,
All but Elizabeth. Outside the door
She spoke to him: 'Would you not like to be
Grown-up? I would.' Paul laughed: 'What would you do,
If you were, Liz?' She blushed, 'I'd marry you,'
And looked defiant love into his eyes.
His right-hand fingers gripped the jamb, 'Poor Liz,
When that time comes I'll be a priest of God.'
Then in a rage she slammed the door on more
Than flesh and bone.

Now in a classroom
Of the Christian Brothers' school for boys sits Paul,
A pedagogue quite undisturbed by dreams.
But when a classroom door is sudden slammed,
Or when at early Mass where the grey nuns sit
His dull eyes light upon Elizabeth,
He grips as if in pain the maimed right hand
That never held a monstrance to a crowd
And marvels in his mind the ways of God.

THE BAIT

She ripples through the silent water, gold
In sunlight, silver underneath the moon;
And even as they look she disappears
Although the land-locked pond in which she swims
Has not a cranny where a carp can hide.

Evasive of their searching fingers, quite
Impervious to their stones, and spurning all
The baited hooks, she moves through watery time
Mysterious and aloof, and waits a prince
Who has not come to cast his lure at last.

For though one snap of jaw would change her mouth
To lips, her fishy parts to flesh, her scales
To golden hair — to break that binding spell
A man must bait his hook with his live heart
And no man yet has had the faith to dare.

SPRING FEVER

As some who are sleek and fed
Envy with truth
The sweet first taste of bread
To a starved mouth,

So I, wedded to joy,
Go hungering
To walk like a love-starved boy
With a girl in Spring.

THE BLUE BIRD

floating through the violet night
beneath the flow of neon stars
here and there an asteroidal face
drew me to its wanderings

a corner turned and these dissolved
and there was only one and she was changed to bird
and to my skin the hue and texture of the feathers
was the blue, tide-breasted sea

How do you know, wrote William Blake, *but ev'ry bird*
that cuts the airy way
is an immense world of delight
closed by your senses five

Blake's words were magic.
I stepped inside the circle of her eyes
to find a world where wish and will were one,
a garden watered by a central sea
and nurtured by an inner sun

my jarring self disturbed the bird of joy
and I was one with Adam, Eve,
Lot's wife, and Orpheus,
alone outside the timeless world

now in the sky
a wingless blue bird floats
on the moonlit gauze of dreams

through the locked orbit of the crowd
I trail the wings she lent me
and look for eyes whose mirror-guards are down

POET

desperate for balance
he walked with his hands
a paper treadmill
over the edge
of his topsy-turvy life
and dared not pause
lest he fall

we who see only
his marks on the paper
praise him for energy
find in his agility
the rhythms of a happy dance

THE BEAUTY OF BROKEN TEETH

Some things are beautiful
or they are not beautiful
as they are used

hands that heal or hands that clench
lips that kiss or lips that curse

Let us consider teeth

There is nothing, I think,
quite so beautiful as broken teeth
when tough guys use them
to pull nails out of women's flesh
impaled on the cross
of our most masculine morality

But this is a pure beauty
that exists only in imagination

Tough guys do not use their teeth for that

PORTRAIT OF A MIDDLE-AGED WOMAN WITH SCAR

the beauty that she grasped at
was white and blazed
like heated steel

that was thirty years ago

now its shape and colour
are dead and smooth
upon her hand

but in her brain
there is no scar

there still the fire burns
and eats her days and nights
with fear

TAVERN SCENE: THE OLD ATHLETE

"I was a-laying them, boy,
long before you were born —"
The old man tells me
all about the sex he'd had
and his wax face softens
in a wrinkled leer
while I listen politely
and sip his beer

I'm glad though that his blear eyes
do not face the street
and the wide-open door
by which the lovers
swing locked and proud
silhouette after silhouette
in the ageless air

IN THE BAR

I saw a man
with a glass of wine
before him on the table

For an hour he gazed
caressing with his eyes
the red rich glow

At last he raised it
near to his lips
then turned and walked away

THE CHEAT

Twenty-six minutes and thirty-four seconds after the late movie
A child was conceived in a double-bed in Fredericton.
Rock Hudson was the proper name of its real father,
And the proper name of its real mother was Jennifer Jones
Although the bodies of Jane and Cyrus Goodfellow
Six years five days and fifteen hours married
Participated as proxies in a double adultery
Arranged by a most respectable sponsor.

VINCENT VAN GOGH

out from the canvas
without ceasing, still life pours
a man's energy

fiery lines leap
in the brain and colours burn
when our eyes are closed

BESIDE THE LAKE

Beside the lake, the grass was tender as
The adolescent sun of spring, the fluff
Of willow-pollen hung upon the air.

Our supple bodies strained to break the cloth
Whose rough, dry fibres kept firm flesh from flesh
That tingled with the swollen veins of spring.

But through that timeless tense the frail strands held
Intact the unseen fabric of a dream
Of honour dyed the same in separate homes,
And when the sunlight waned at last we left,
Unmated still in all that mating world.

Today I stood alone beside the lake
And wondered where that boy and girl had gone.

INSIDE THE ROOM'S ELECTRIC AIR

Inside the room's electric air
we watched two birds alight
on high-tension wires and sing

I turned to her and spoke,
"If their wing-tips touched
they'd both go up in flames."

She looked at me and reached
to take in mine her burning hands

THE GUEST

Like a god he is —
while there's a listener left
and the liquor lasts.

SUN FUGUE

slow and under
the waveless depths, and cold
amid the gold sea
anemones
crawls the starfish still
whose only nerve is
appetite. How far
did the star crawl
in the gone centuries?

over the brackish waters
of a new-made world
the sun as father brooded
and when the clouds dispersed
it was his light that stung
the starfish into life.
O Stella Maris!
O Star of the Sea!

but in those chill depths
the rays too dimly shone
and white flesh that longed
to feed upon
the gift of gold
soon nerved itself
to prey, and fed
to get the sun
a quicker way
and preying, feeding still
toward the sun
the starfish crawled
and gulped the radiant air
with lungs at last.

then in light's plenitude
the slow crawl quickened
danced and flew
and mind became

a higher kind
of chlorophyll
as parasitic hunger
softened with the kiss
of light on lofty cliffs
where cruel wings dipped
to down of gold . . .

the urge to give beyond the skin
became so strong
that sun-won love
betrayed the sun
to bring again
the fleshly hunger
of the crawling star
more lethal from
the grace and ease
that air had won.

cleaving the blue, white
gulls with the grace of heaven
winnow the windless air
over the glass-blue waters
untarnished by
the shadow of a cloud
they hover, seeking fish.

A BETRAYAL

words keep their own truths

to all other things
they are a betrayal

like this poem I made

out of our silent touch

THE LOVERS' NEEDS DISSOLVE

the lovers' needs dissolve
the surfaces they let each other see

now they have become a will-less wave
of swelling nerves and blood
afloat on that dark element
which spoke in flesh before the word was made

how will it be when each returns
to the sand and puny kingdom
whose horizon is the separate self?

THE CAGE

At times the bird inside the cage
Is very dear to me.
At times my thoughts go with the bird
That flies alone and free.

Should I let loose the bird I have
To coax the wild one here
Such change of roles would only make
The other one more dear.

Without the cage I cannot want
Or love or think or say;
Its barriers limn the forms of life
As sun-spokes shape the day.

FOR FORTY-EIGHT YEARS NOW

For forty-eight years now
I have been saying I — what
have I been saying?

DIARY ENTRY

Today I wrote three letters
but did not send them

I bear the fetters
of a double pain,
the hurt she gave
and the greater hurt
I refuse to give

Still too human
to be noble
how shall I let her know?

THE BOTTLE DUNGEON:
SAINT ANDREW'S, SCOTLAND

a land-fish caught
in the Christian depths —
the black cold net
of the bottle dungeon
where Saint Andrew's monks
had chilled the heretics
of burning centuries —
upward I burst,
gasping for heat and light.

on the solid floor
of the blood-warmed element
I scanned my airy globe
for comfort and for calm.

a gold-beaked gull
stared back at me
with implacable eyes
and his white wings made
a Saint Andrew's cross
against the October sky.

DIRECTION

by the black lines
of a street-map
I travel this city,
recalling no north
south east or west
in its fragmented sky

but when I go
back to the place
where my heart grew
the sky inside my head
I move as birds move
when they fly

A NICE QUESTION

on the lake, the sky
in calm trust will often let
her fair image lie

but never allow
the thick-surfaced lake to print
his shape upon her

is sky's purity
or her levity the cause
of this imbalance?

BUT SOMETIMES RISING

when I close my eyes
a deep ocean swells to drown
the dry shapes of day

but sometimes rising
in the waters of my mind
flesh faces waver

into clarity —
tantalizing cameos
like quicksilver fish

that gleam and vanish
as the current twists and shifts,
or mermaids groping

from the wrong side of
time's translucent element
for what might have been

THE WAITING TIME

I

bird-notes twinkle through
the waiting time, in and out
like stars through grey cloud

II

fingers touch the tree
its young trunk is firm and cool
white like moonlit skin

III

now all the evening
holds its dusky breath and waits
why do you not come?

IV

a stone in the path
moves . . . each ear's a hound to pounce
but it is not you

THE GIRL I LOVE IS FLESH AND BLOOD

The girl I love is flesh and blood,
Stands five feet six at most,
Throws tantrums when she's crossed
And does not do the things she should.

I know her eyes are merely eyes,
Her touch like mine is skin,
And yet when I begin
To touch and look these truths turn lies

And she becomes the living sum
Of all the dreams that fed
My lonely nights in bed
When desire was locked and dumb.

And that is why my pride has gone,
And why I gnaw these days
Her few lean scraps of praise
As a famished dog his bone.

FISH-DINNER

though fish-knives keep
ceremonial shape
fish bring no fear
to eaters here

fish slim and straight
on the full-moon plate
as lances trail
across a grail

fish from the dread
deeps of the dead
salt element
the dove's complement

now our calm jaws mesh
on blood and flesh
mindless of the bride
of the life-giving tide

for Astarte's gone
and Leviathan
the drier Christ
tamed to Eucharist . . .

but still in our blood
the life-tides flood
as the monthly moon
makes real the myths of men

THE TRICK OF FAITH

"Shut your eyes," Paul said,
"Press your eyelids hard
And you will see
Round wheels of gold
Inside your head."

I tried, but all
I saw was just plain black.

I told him so.

"You don't press hard enough".
He said,
"It takes a lot of pain
To make it work."

I tried once more — no wheels.

Besides, the pressure
Made my eyelids ache.

MONISM

Where river slides through spreading thighs of soil
Whose maidenhead is captured by the worm,
Where summer air wins free from tension's coil
As lightning darts to deepest womb of storm
Its thrust of terror and of beauty home,
I look around me and my senses reel
To see the universe outside become
A mirror of the passion that I feel.

Where jetting fountains into basins run,
Where mountains thrust hard heads through yielding cloud,
Where Lombard poplars straighten in the sun,
Where grass springs phallic from the fleshly shroud
And stubborn root rapes bone till bone is gone,
The world grows crystal clear in terms of form
As micro-macrocosmic shapes make one
Recurring symbol of the mated norm.

And there stream, worm, air, tree, mount, grass, and root
Am I; you are all complements to these;
And each relation, articulate or mute,
Is ours; and should death end our entities
These cells in other forms will dance the same;
Whether in galaxies or the mind's rooms
In unity unfolds the endless game
Of egg-and-dart all energy assumes.

THIS PAPER ONCE BREATHED

In bud and leaf and twig
this paper once breathed

Tonight it speaks
my life to you

TO DEIRDRE

Deep buried in my body's need and fed
From loam of all those fertile lines
That poets delved in days
When what is dust was blood and bone,
You grew, a tall and shadowy tree
In the wood of my wild blood,
Though even then the you I glimpsed
Held shape enough to cool and form
My adolescent dreams.

Now I have known you, I have seen
Behind your fair, translucent flesh
The outlines of a free and honest self
That moves at ease where I am most afraid.
What wonder then I hoard you now
Inside my memory's battered purse
As a miser guards a minted coin
Of sharp and shining gold?

But I would throw both coin and purse
Against the face of time
To feel once more the tumult in the wood
When sunbeams caught the inner vein
And turned the scalding touch of fire
Into soft hands of green-gold light
Beneath a maze of leaves, of lovely lines,
The not-impossible-growth of dreams.

THE BUTTERFLY

For years I hunted butterflies and looked with pride
on rows of set and labelled wings
that slowly faded underneath the glass.

Today by chance or whim one rare and beautiful
swooped down to light upon my open palm.
I did not close my fist.

A TRIAD

I

Birds by the water,
your notes unheard mid sweeter
sings of human flesh,

now I hear you sing
though all the lake is frozen
fast and you are flown

II

Sweet-grass in the dark,
your touch and smell once smothered
by a woman's hair

are fresh as summer
in my nose and fingers though
you have long decayed

III

Plums in the orchard
unsavoured when her tart red
lips eclipsed your own

I can taste you now
though you lie brown and rotting
under drifts of snow

THE SENSES

My mind opens the windows of my eyes
and I see you standing straight and clear
although you are
                    miles and years away

When memory moves the inner ear
deep inside

I hear your voice
and smile with sudden joy

And sometimes in a vacant room
the familiar scent of you
                              now and then
as from a flower breathes

But what my mind loves most
the touch and taste of you
                              is dead
except through masks of other women

THEY SCARCELY DARED TO TOUCH

They scarcely dared to touch
the earth of stone and cinder
for fear its dirt would smutch
love's feet so white and tender

But now relaxed they know
how vain was that fine caring
to whom love's an old shoe
that fits better with wearing.

THE WOUND AND THE SCAR

The wound is closed,
the hurt is gone,
as water closes
over a plunging stone;

but the scar it leaves
still proves to me
hearts are not water
whatever stone may be.

LIKE TWO SLANT TREES

"Lean on me," he said,
loving her weakness

and she leaned hard
adoring his strength

Like two slant trees
they grew together

their roots the wrong way
for standing alone

IN THE MORNING COLD

in the morning cold
I woke by the lake alone
and a sharp reed said:

"Your happiness is
water for the sun to dry
and all that beauty

reflected from her
a wisp of cloud that any
wind can blow away."

AFTER YOU LEFT ME

after you left me I stood
silent on grey stones

and watched while a deaf
and dumb tree talked to the wind
with fluttering hands

UNDER THE WILLOW

Under
the willow where
the falling pollen
powdered your face
I think of the first
wind that blew
on the first willow
by this lake

the air
scarcely swayed
the stamens as it passed
but that pollen-touch
a billion winds ago
sired the shade
of our desperate
brief embrace

that first
tree never cared
where the wanton
wind had gone
nor does this now
remember her ghostly father
as she feeds
on her mother's mould

how much kinder than lovers
do they meet and part
in the green-blood world

THE DIFFERENCE

Oak cannot remove
its mistletoe — but I can,
O my clinging love!

A LOVER'S CATECHISM

L. What is the first need of love?
   The first need of love is acceptance.
2. What should the lover accept?
   The lover should accept the worlds that
   are given him to love. He should accept
   them as they are: who prunes the rose
   of its thorns does not love the rose.
3. How is acceptance made manifest?
   Acceptance is made manifest by toleration.
   Reformers never love what they wish to
   alter.
4. What in theory are the limits of love?
   The entire universe of apprehendible
   being is in theory the limit of love.
5. What in practice ought to be the limits of love?
   In practice, love should be limited to
   what lies within the nature and situation
   of the lover to apprehend and love.
6. What should be the attitude of the lover toward
the universe that lies outside the practical limits
of his love?
   Insofar as he has time and opportunity,
   the lover should draw as much of existence
   as he can into his universe; otherwise it
   should remain to him as a thing indifferent.
7. Is there a hierarchy of love?
   There are as many hierarchies of love as
   there are lovers, and the relations between
   them ought always to be like those that
   exist between peers.
8. What is the fruit of love?
   Love's fruit is energy.
9. How is this energy displayed?
   Love of the earth is displayed in heart-beat
   and breath; love of a man or a woman in the
   sexual embrace; love of one's self in contemplation
   and thought.

10. What then are painting, sculpture, music, and
    poems in relation to love?
        These things are the masks that memory
        creates to hide the failure of love. Its
        success requires meither shape nor sound.

PERSPECTIVE

Like a moth whose vision dwindles
To one clear point of fire
My passion bent the universe
To the form of its desire.

Now free at last I gaze, my eye
Content to look alone:
How lovely is the varied world
I have no wish to own.

TO A ROSE

Your fragrance after
the stranger took you from me
became my heart's thorn.

His delight is sweet.
Sweet to me this pain. O Rose,
you are not wasted.

WINTER

in another's arms
you sleep . . . heavy lies the snow
on our summer bed

BEHIND THE BLOOD

I do not know the blood
        that feeds my own
        most healthy parts

and should a power supply
        the pulse of blood
        as blood feeds me

how could my intellect
        probe inwardly
        to reach that god

for all the senses turn
        to measure things
        beyond control

the universe outside
        that makes a constant
        discord to my will?

this world is lasting, large
        and I am small
        I make images

of the order that I find
        in season, sun
        and moon and star

and try to use their power
        to give me ease
        from pain and death

and when they do not work
        I peer inside
        my self for flaws

and when they work I praise
        and never look
        behind the blood

where God might move in me
    so perfect that
    I would not know

STAR-PEOPLE

In all shapes and sizes do they walk the earth
As men and women wherever men and women are;
How can we know them? How can we tell
Beneath what skin unfolds the petals of a star?

They eat and drink and love and hate like men.
Like men they're prone to colds and shirk their tasks.
So well they ape the human-robots in their moves
That they at times forget they're wearing masks.

But when they meet another of their kind,
Underneath the current of their usual words
There chimes, inaudible to human ears,
Bell-music like the cries of mating birds.

And when they touch the other's hands or eyes
Such joys along their nerve-ways race
They scarce can bear to smile and make small-talk
As though no miracle were taking place.

THE CAGED GULL

Though light you lift
against the breeze,
cleaving blue sky
with white-winged ease,

here, too, you live,
o eye-caught gull —
caged in a small
mnemonic skull

LINES FOR MY FIFTIETH BIRTHDAY

"...old age serene and bright,
And lovely as a Lapland night."
— William Wordsworth

money's to spend,
strength is to use,
pleasure's to have
again and again
till the nerves refuse

let the middle-aged
take the middle way,
save, guard, and pray;
in love, work, or play
the young have no use
for husbandry —
to them Aristotle's rule
is more mean than gold

they are one with the old

I shall be a fire
of what I am and have
and burn till I expire
in the free air of love;
only the uncombining
unresurrectionable part
shall rot in the grave

let them bury me sans skin
sans eyes sans nose sans mouth
sans ears sans arms sans brain
sans penis and sans heart

THE DEBT I OWE THE BOOKS

they taught dimensions
until all that had seemed
so separate and still
was linked in flow
of moving patterns

I saw the sun
shoot electric life
into the womb-sky of heaven
and its rhythms danced
with blinding light

and here and there
a gaseous ovary
was ripe to hold
the darting sperm,
some in nightmare shapes
of abortive life
and some in forms
made viable for growth

these last, I saw
were cannibals
upon their kin,
stealing the parent-life
from other cells

and yet each bore
a minor sun,
a lesser womb;
and two combined
could create
with more economy
than any star

emancipating walls
of wood or chitin,
horn, skin, or scale,
defied the parent power,

admitting only
however much of sun
as warmed and fed
their sea-found blood

but cell-armour
was not perfect
and in crevices
decay and death
waited to come in

this made the worth
of living heighten
into sentient selves
that loved their cells
and fought to keep
them all alive

historic time . . .
where lust for life
and fear of death
combined to form
a greater, lasting
group-cell cluster
in which despised
necessity became
the chosen ways
of mutual love
as each in other
saw a mirror of
his social self
and with a wealth
of symbols filled
a new one-world

there the mind creates,
expanding and contracting
all the metaphors
of time and space,
of shape and motion

and the hates and loves
of history,
applying all things
to its own needs
in eccentric rhythms
of the moment's harmony

and so the books
have opened, and although
I am as much
a child as any child
who cannot read
as to why the things
should be that are,
the debt I owe
the books is this:
the books have taught me
not to be afraid

MAKING POEMS IS LIKE

making poems is like
making love

there is no end
no finished product

only a series
of possibilities

where performance
breaks the heart of desire

with here and there
worth all the rest

a lucky accident
in which the two are one

THE SMILE

Across the living room
he smiles his smile. That smile
to you is Moby Dick,
the bland and rosy mask
the universe assumes
to hide the fact that it
is callous to your will
and wounding, maiming, cruel.

Then all your wounds reburn
and you, like Ahab, launch
your venom at the source
of life-frustrating power,
but every time you rip
the mask away you find
it covers something quite
as wretched as yourself.

FOR THIS WITH ECSTASY

Somewhere the sun
smiles on your face

and smooth hands of air
caress your skin

For this with ecstasy
I embrace the wind

and turn my eyes
to the full light

BACCHANAL

geometric
sky hangs
stars in grooves
and day round
with constant course
Apollo's car
dispenses light

earth shapes
the fluid sea
recoils
in waves that take
their wedge
form from the one
wind sky lets blow

but Chthon, the cave
where light not
shine, where black
blots stars and lids
eclipse round
eyes in night
mare sleep
sweat-cold and coupled
foul with beasts
or crushed by bone-
less snakes of slime
smeared flesh
that grinning wears
a parent's face

the boundless
power seeps
through the planed
universe to the sick
child that grows
to god on blood
and wine, crying
in me, crying
"evoe! evoe!"

FLOWER-GIRL

"Here's a flower for you
you sad old man"--
and she pinned it
to my lapel

I did not want
the flower
nor did I covet
the brighter bloom
of her form and face

what I wanted was
the white diamond
of her spirit
that the ugliness
of St. Catherine Street
could not abrade

MARIJUANA TEA

The lines and coloured squares
dance on the wall
to the intricate beat
of record-rhythms
and through the marijuana's
sting of smoke
the party oohs and ahs
and sips its china tea

I sip it and I savour
the one sense
by "pot" made keener

Of a sudden
I remember
the cold of oatmeal

sugar and well-water
in the dusty haymow
after the last load
had been stowed away

how good that tasted
how happy-tired
and relaxed I was

TIED WOLF

fierce eyes, steel chain,
and tortured skin --
the tethered wolf
and I are kin --
he fastened fast
to mindless steel,
I to the grasp
of my own will.

GRAIL

though all life since
has seemed but shadows
of an untouched light

I am a lucky man . . .

some heve never seen
a holy grail

others don't believe
that one exists

SOLILOQUY

when you are here, my mind assembles
refracted light the eyes receive
from whatsoever place wherein
you stand or sit or lie or kneel

and closer and more delicate
nerve-fingers weave the subtle shape
of texture and of temperature
and the electric thrill of touch

these things the words you write and say
are stored in cells that fuse in time
with aspects of my wish and will
to make the sum of what you are

yet other shapes form other myths
one I scorn is by another loved
as you my dear are scorned by some
how much of what we see is us?

is love a drawing to those things
that come to us and somehow fit
our narrow appetites for form?
is hate a discord in our dreams?

who shaped the dream I am and when,
what matters when I only know
the myths I make are true within,
grow parts that I must love or hate?

we are all fishermen. Narcissus
fished only in a shallow pond
and caught his own reflection
to feed the time's monotony

I love to fling the sensual net
in the world's sea -- and from that draw in
exotic food my brain digests
to grow a second self called you

THE SAD PHOENIX

whether we have wedded
license to be bedded
or you be whore
and I adulterer
it is all one
when we lie close and dumb
in each other's arms

when I touch you I become
the you I touch as much
as you grow me and when
our quick of oneness blooms
in nervous flame
why then its fire consumes
alike the dross and gold

so for a while we hold
a pure and blending fire;
but from its ashes rise
thorny tongues of pride
that split the self once more
to husband, wife,
adulterer, and whore

THE LOVES OF THE EYE

caught in the light's shimmering net
out of the fathomless waters of sky
from the salmon flesh of morning
to the starfish schools of night
the loves of the eye

so adjusted is their flow
to all the ways in which I move
that I must bless the wantonness
with which they seem to come and go
these beauties that I cannot grasp and own

STRIVE NEVER WITH WORDS

Strive never with words to arc the impossible span,
Building a bridge of poems where straight through
                  the gate of her eye
Your mind can move to hers in a closer longer embrace
Than that of lust-driven lovers who peril both body
                  and love;

For words, however solid they seem, are shadowy shapes
                  to the real
And though flesh that casts no shadow may be evil
                  and damned
The shadow that mixes with shadow regardless of flesh
Is only an ape in the guise of God raping the soul . . .

Let there be no one-way going in the giving and taking
Where shadow and flesh are discarded as clumsy and slow,
Let your love so spring from your eyes that hers in
                  responding
Will meet it and fuse in the beautiful silence of light.

THEIR GIANT LIVES

we drew into our emptiness
the deadly fungus of the dead

black spores of type inside our eyes
took root to sap our blood and brains

their clinging tendrils tied our flesh
till it assumed a pygmy form

and to the world we never faced
we said: "Bow down before these men,

they put in books to feed us all
the marrow of their giant lives."

TO MARTHA

we all love you,
Martha-woman,
who to all men are
most mother-human

your patient womb
unbars its gate
whether we tender woo
or, raping, hate

nothing we are
affects your breast
that gives us fondling, food,
or velvet rest

and so you crumble
all our love--deeds, sense,
made void of meaning
by your obedience

then in revenge
our souls take flight
to any Mary
of the painted night

who, having roused
our atavistic urges,
will pay us back
with whips and scourges.

MIRACLES

. . . a green leaf clinging
to a winter bough . . . and you,
incredible love

DON JUAN'S LAST TRIUMPH

"Yes, Don Juan, take your time," the devil said.
"Your fate depends on how you answer me."

I take my time and see my life flash by:
A blur of female flesh, plump painted birds
That fell before my male hypnotic gaze
And left their plumage in the trophy rooms
Of memory. I feel the hunting pride,
The surge of power that fed on victory
And gave all games a zest I never queried.
And then I see the Donna Helen's eyes
And hear the "No" come firmly from her lips.
So clear I see that look and hear that voice
I know that his satanic majesty
Who waits in patience for my answer now
Can not torment me as that woman did.
What's in a look? What's in a word? you say.
Why, if the devil only knew he'd die,
Finding himself and all infernal tricks
Alike redundant. Looks and words are lens
That turn a view of heaven into hell.
What did I learn from Donna Helen's then?
The wisdom that the echo learns when first
It is aware the pealing bell exists,
Its small importance in the scheme of things.
She was a woman and not moved by me.
Therefore the force to move lay not in me
But in her self, and then I knew
That this was truth in all my women known:
What moved them was their own hot fires held in
Too long, and not the heat that blazed in me,
And I was dross to feed those hellish flames,
And Helen, being pure, could only burn
On better tinder than the thing I was.
But shall I tell the devil all of this?
He is the Don Juan of souls. It would,
I fear, deflate his thin balloon of pride
To know that power's not in him but in

His victims. "Twere kind to let him triumph, go
To hell and spare him what I suffer now.

"My lord, I'll say no words in my defence.
I ask no mercy. Work your will on me."

FISHERMEN

with the rod of the law
in his claw
God casts his luring fly
of beauty
over a deep, blind pool

that every fool
of pink-flesh desire
may wriggle and squirm
and feel like a worm
with a gutful of fire
on a hook of steel

these form a sky
and under it sly
flabby and cold
the wise fish wait

their cruel jaws snap
on all who drop
as they lose their hold
on heaven's bait

HAIKU

wind-blown daffodils
wink in a water-blue bowl
gold fish light the pool

ASPECTS OF MATERIALISM: I

. . . a mindless odyssey
over a wind-waved, green
and starling-perilled sea

halts in a spun-silk screen
hammock slung in a dry
harbour, and then the lean,

slow grub, now butterfly,
from an unremembered wave
of cabbages climbs high

on fragile wings to brave
brief mating in the sky
then drops to seed a grave

beneath the meadow sea
that flesh may plod again
a mindless odyssey . . .

THE WHIP OF LOVE

grief when you gave it
was sweet
and I was happy
despite the hurt

now you no longer
punish me
I feel all the other
whips set free

lord, if in suffering
I must live
let it be under
the whip of love

MYTH

when Proteus fled
from his cold shell
cathedral
on the salt sea's bed

his liquid stride
over the sand
quickened the land
to a greener pride

till up from the loam
in velvet motion
a grassy ocean
curled in fragrant foam

CARTRIDGE COLLECTOR

The last to know what all the neighbours knew,
When Frank discovered that his slattern wife
Was taking lovers on the sly, his life
Went on almost as though she still were true.

He never spoke to let her know he knew
But ate and slept with her and paid each bill,
Bought toys for birthdays, just as if he still
Were sure her children were his children too.

Only his hobby held him more and more—
So much he told his friends about the ways
And makes of shells that he became a bore:
Then all alone—the box upon his knees—
He'd sit and fondle one by one and gaze
Upon a pile of empty cartridges.

DEMOCRACY

Joe Benson and his wife would fight and smash
The windows of the small tarpaper shack
They lived in right behind the railway track
Then make it up, and if they had the cash,
They'd both of them get drunk on bootleg mash
And stay that way until their money went.
Unless they earned it, no one gave a cent
To them who always were and would be trash.

But suddenly a day would come when she
Was given credit at the Elder's store
While Sunday-suited men in cars would go
And dare the mud before the shanty door,
Trying with money, drink, and flattery
To buy Joe's vote, worth more to them than Joe.

MOLLIE JONES

When Tom came in and saw the dishes piled
Up in the sink, his waiting supper cold,
He did not stop to nag at her or scold
But ate and washed and dried them all and smiled
His sad, slow patient smile that drove her wild;
And when she told him she was going out that night
He looked at her and said, "My dear, all right;
Have a good time," as though she were a child.

She hates him for his namby-pamby ways.
If he'd get drunk and beat her up some days
Or have himself a woman now and then,
Come home to swear at her and call her bitch
She'd like far more her fun with other men
Who are more lively loving and more rich.

WILLIAM CAIN

When William Cain came back to Centreville
The first time since the day he left his people
He found that storms had halved the Baptist steeple
And a spring flood had carried off the mill

And though he found a few old sweethearts still,
Each apple cheek he once had pressed his lip in
Was puckered like a sour Winter Pippin
In which the worms of time had worked their will.

But sadder somehow in these meetings was
The sudden thought that took him unaware:
How high-arched feet that danced upon the grass
Or raced along the roadways brown and bare
Had sagged beneath the growing weight of care
To plod flat-footed like a spavined mare.

JOE ANGUS

Joe Angus was a good man with an axe;
A silent man, who, if you knew, you'd feel
Had but one tongue and that of hardened steel
That slow and easy wagged when he was lax.
His swing was clean and smooth. He timed his hacks
To suit his temper, but go rile him good
And he'd lash out against the stubborn wood
That gave like cheese before his strongest whacks.

When his wife nagged him, he great gashes made,
And mighty were the curling chips that fell
When his two boys got drunk. But men still say
That when they told him, one October day,
How his girl had run off with a ne'er-do-well,
He stared without a word and dropped his blade.

LILY JONES

At Tompkins house that stood beside the river
She used to go to Pentecostal meeting:
They'd start by singing hymns with both feet beating
Till the rhythms of the music made them shiver

Then Brother Strong God's message would deliver
While all the time the movement of the Spirit
Was pulling them till they could hardly bear it
But straining sat with all their souls a-shiver.

Then some would rise up, shouting, "Glory, glory,
Hallelujah!" while other ones would dance
Or talk in tongues as in the Gospel Story;
But though she saw their souls like rubber bands
Go snapping as they slipped the clasp of ill
The Glory and the Power never came to Lil.

T. V. WATCHER

Soft in her chair she sees the visions bloom
And needs no prince to wake her drowsy flesh.
Soft on her screen she sees the patterns mesh
Of rugged males whose scowling passions loom
With two-gunned violence in her living-room.
Oh, how she loves them, aches to share their throes,
Her feelings sharp and variable as those
Who move in monochrome a switch can doom.

She will not flick it off for flesh and blood.
Where can she give so little, gain so much,
Be heroic without risk, diet without food,
Adventure safely in the bleak outdoors,
Have lovely children without household chores,
And thrill to love untarnished by a touch?

EPISODE

When first our bodies rolled
And crushed the pollen-gold
That fell from apple boughs
In blossom-drunk carouse,
We muffled up the seeds
Of our fear-convicted deeds
And doomed our lovers' spring
To sterile blossoming.

But now in Summer-heat
When scarlet fruit grows sweet
On unrepentent trees,
We turn our eyes from these
And pry beneath the mould
To watch the slugs with cold
And slimed veracity
Feed on dead loves that lie.

CRITIC

the wings of butterflies
disclose no mysteries

their beauty is but powdered dust
that hides familiar membranes

DAILY TEXT

The men who nailed God's flesh
To the bitter tree
Were merely earning wages
Like you and me.

LESSON IN AESTHETICS

This page has now
two fields of force
one white (potential)
one black (kinetic)
thickly populated
by these my words

as I write them down
the white diminishes
and the black field grows

the first refracts
your mind like light
but this other
is your eyes' flypaper

however your mind-wings
flutter or buzz
you are trapped, reader,
by no great beauty
nor emotive force
nor the strange dance
of images

the simple battern
of two-beat lines
and your most human
desire to know
where it is they lead
has brought you
to this end

IMMORTAL PLOWMAN

His footsteps waver
In the clay, but each furrow
that he turns is straight

CIRCULAR SAWS

When the circular saw
chewed up my fingernail
I said to myself
"This is a bad dream
and I shall wake up"
but I didn't
and in a few minutes
the pain began

after that, I had
a scar to remind me
not to go near
circular saws

But I soon found
they had ways
of disguising themselves
so that watch as I might
they were always
hurting me

now inside and out
I am covered with scars
but that is not
the worst I've learned
the worst thing is
that under the masks
I wear and without
intending to be
I am a circular saw

LOVE

. . . as he rushed toward
her outstretched arms, his toe crushed
a ground-sparrow's nest

THE WIND AND THE TREE

That Spring the gnarled and ancient apple tree,
Feeling the May wind's kiss, unfurled
Green leaves like flags to greet the sun, and all
Its crown grew white with blossom where great bees
With pollen-dusted fur flew day-long flights
To hive the harvest of the scented boughs.

Now on the Autumn ground the apples lie,
And with them soon will mingle in the mould
The leaves whose edges even now are brown
With death; for deadlier than the keenest axe
The kiss of too much living drove the tree
To greater harvest than its back could bear.

A kissing wind that did not dream its power,
A tree that could not feel the limits of
Its all too feeble strength--by chance the two
Combined. The end their union formed was fruit.
But which of us who dreams and feels can say
Whether the end of fruit be life or death?

A HUMAN CONDITION

they raised
smooth walls around him
front and back and side

each wall
as mirror magnified
his naked gross desires

till he ate
from garish packages
their cheap, alluring dreams

TOM FOOL'S LUCK

Tom Fool was lucky in the women
    whom he picked to love:
They preferred the active vice
    of other men
To all the negative virtue
    that shone in him.

OBITUARIES

I look at obituaries

what interests me
are the figures
that tell me
the ages of the dead

If the ones I see
are less than mine
I am forced to stifle
a quick thrill of joy
at having outlived
a fellow human

If the number
I read is greater
I rejoice to think
of all the years
a man like me
can look forward to

but when the age
written there
is the same as mine
I shudder and wish
that there were no
obituaries

IN PRAISE OF CHASTITY

There was a girl once . . .

I remember her
because she wore
the very same dress
to school every day

it was white and old
and out-of-date
but somehow
it fitted her so well
that none of us boys
ever thought
of taking it off
or how she would look
in another dress

and after we saw
the shine in her eyes
and the light in her face
we liked her so much
the way she was
that we wouldn't have dared
to change a thing about her
even if we could

THE CAMERA-EYE

the pulses of the sun
transmit in rhythmic flow
the shimmering waves of light
that flood the camera-eye

by what strange solution
fixed and developed
in the brain's dark room
are they preserved as form?

WELL-PINNED AND SET

well-pinned and set
in my study lies
a cabinet
of butterflies,

the shards of what
I cannot keep
in living thought:
the eager leap,

the painted toy
not seen before,
now mine--my joy
there in a jar

while I breathed, in air
outside and free,
all my human share
of eternity

which was to forget
in present bliss
the limits set
on being. All this

is gone. Now here,
myself in a jar,
the prisoner
of things that are,

I breathe time's fumes,
the lethal gas
that fills up rooms
where interests pass,

and count it boon
few cells survive
to feel the pin
that death may drive.

IN THIS DREAM

In this dream
                she was
all the different
                    kinds of women
I ever met
and I
     a bloodless ghost
whose only form
                was her face
in the daily mirror

Seen from the eye
                  or camera-lens
it was the smooth gloss
                    of beauty

but the trapped
              male ego
felt the invisible
              web
and fought
           and screamed

THE DARK STILL WORLD OF SLEEP

Domestic love is calm and good
As kindness brings the daily food
On which we grow more sleek and fat
And like a cat we purr our thanks;

But in the dark still world of sleep
Another Eros conjures ghosts
With hungry eyes that hardly fade
Before the x-ray sanity of light.

AN UNRELEASE

out of the nerve-swarm
and the mind-jar
we met to form
a double star

on whose orbits peace
is one with love--
an unrelease
where two worlds move

that cannot reach
yet may not part,
each held to each
by its magnetic heart

THE POMEGRANATES

After Paul Valery

Hard pomegranates burst to ease
The pressure of your ripened grains,
In you I see majestic brains
Explode with their discoveries!

If all the force of all the suns,
O pomegranates half-split wide,
Created you with studied pride
To crack your red partitions,

And if the dry gold of your skin
At the call of a force within
Shatters in scarlet gems of juice,

That clear and meaningful rupture
Compels the soul I am to muse
Upon its secret architecture.

IN VAIN YOU BUILD YOUR WOOD OF WORDS

In vain you build your wood of words
That you inviolate still
May reign—despite those brambled swords
I'll conquer when I will;

For in the chamber of your eye
Where none may forests make
I see a naked princess lie,
Waiting her cue to wake.

A LETTER

After you wandered dazedly
To escape my storm of angry words
And vanished round the cliff
That overhangs the sand
I walked beside your footsteps,
Accommodating every stride
To suit the pace you took.
And where you stopped
And, turning, blurred the ground
I did the same
And carefully discarded
A half-smoked cigarette
To match each one you threw away.

I'm glad I did those things
Although I am quite certain
That, were you there, our quarrel
Had still gone on.

Afterward I walked the beach
Before the tide came in with one
Who said: "Here two lovers came.
See how their footsteps wandered
Yet kept together as though

The only point of reference
In all the wavering world
Was how each one to the other was.
See how he waited on her lagging steps
See how she inward leaned
To make with him
An arch against the world."

Such faith, my dear, he had
In evidence. Yet who was I
To say that he was wrong?

THE GIANT INN

when vision pierced the nightmare fog
illusion-thin
they saw themselves as prisoners
in a giant inn

where each man down at table sat
with his heaped plate
and each man turned to skeleton
the while he ate

their throats grew parched and dumb
from swallowing
but one girl from her own red blood
drank strength to sing

all famine-lean they grew as they
munched meat and bread
though one who gnawed his own raw heart
was briefly fed

the host brought food and drink to them
from every side
and took no pains to feed himself
he never died

WE ARE ALL LITTLE LAMBS

the cigarette-butts rest
in the crowded ash-trays
and gray wisps of smoke
fade and dissolve
in the empty-glass morning
like ghosts of departed guests

the young engineer
drunk from too much rum and poetry
sleeps on the sofa alone

while the host, the would-be poet,
recites a Shakespeare sonnet
con amore for the only words
that almost say
what no words
can say at all

and the mauve-haired girl
I hold in my arms
snuggles close to my ear
and breathes in her sleep
a name not my own

AN OLD MAN GAZING

an old man gazing
at glow of young flesh whirling
cried, "That is my meat"

forgetting how new
and shiny shoes pinch the corns
of his tired feet.

LYRIC

Be patient, Sweet. Forbear
Your power to keep me true.
O let me laugh a while
With warmer loves than you,

That I may tire at last
Of change which will not cease
And long to trade life's charms
For your one gift of peace.

Come then with kiss that dooms
All other loves that call,
And glad in your embrace
I shall forget them all.

THE DARK WORLD

"We are the hollow men." -- T.S. Eliot

It was not food: we were not hungry.
It was not love: we had that too.
Our surplus rubbed the masks of sense
That covered us and wore them through.

They slipped, and as our minds' clear mirrors
Flashed white to catch the hidden wholes,
We stared aghast at empty air
Where should have shone our living souls.

So all acts turned to joyless shadows
And thoughts grew futile in the mind--
A hollow masquerade of masks
That moved and hid no face behind.

A DILEMMA

the fish in that world of his
can't feel what water is
yet is painfully aware
of air

and since the black and white
that make our moral sight
lets neither man nor woman
be amphibian

therefore it jars my mood
lady, to find you good . . .
what must you think of me?
what must I be?

PICNIC

"Let the poor fish drink," you said,
pouring the red wine
Into the cool river.

"And the ants can have this chicken" —
Into the alder bushes
I flung the hamper.

Ants and fish and summer died.
Chicken warms my winter now
And you drink Beaujolais.

A DEVIL

Who is a devil?
Each man who likes to play God
Without being God.

THE LOG

You lit the log and spoke:

"We do not seek its heat
But it will let us see
The flame we kindle
In each other's flesh."

The log you lit is ash.
Somewhere it feeds green flame
That blazes to the sun
And dances for the wind.

My dear, we did not burn
The log in vain.

INSIDE THE MIGHTY EYE OF PALOMAR

Inside the mighty eye of Palomar
The light is magnified wherever light
Is found--till midnight sky becomes a bright
New world shot through with galaxy and star
Whose image photographed shines nearer far
To universal truth than ever did
The black futility those spaces hid
When eye unaided sought to pierce the bar.

In this magnifying magic science speaks
The self-same message as those men whose rite
Of ancient magic we today deride--
The saints and poets also said: "Who seeks
To pattern truth must magnify the light
In whatsoever dark the light may hide."

SUCH A GOOD GUY

A poet friend once said
"You are such a good guy
That whenever I see
One of your poems
I read it, hoping to find
Something you've written
That I can honestly praise."

When he said this, I wished
I were what he thought I was.

Then I could have tried him out
With a found poem
In which all the lines
Came from his own repertoire.

PARTING

When we were young and shy and good
Beside her father's gate she stood,
Poised like a sleeping tree in June
Though her hands were birds beneath the moon.

Then in the space between us two
Slowly a painful barrier grew
Through which we dared not venture quite,
So I stammered out a lame goodnight.

Strange irony of mental vision:
To me that parting's indecision
Still sharper on my memory lies
Than all love's later certainties.

NEARING THE BEND

after the chance
              swerve and dent
of hit-and-run love
                 her life moved
on the slippery roads
                  of the heart
like the spinning
               useless wheels
of a doomed car
              nearing the bend.

THE LIGHT THAT PIERCED PRIMEVAL SEAS

the light that pierced primeval seas
and drove the lancing sperm
is poisoned now by mysteries,
flesh rose and fleshlier worm;

therefore we blink our modest lids,
the holy beams repress
till darkness comes and custom bids
us decently undress.

PERSPECTIVE

when blinding talons struck
deep through the cells of birth
and the great horror shook
all life out of the earth

along a shining track
without a break in tune
the light danced back
to the man in the moon.

A LIAISON

For a few hours in the evening
he often goes to see her

and she sits with her sewing
while he sits, smoking his pipe

sometimes when their eyes meet
they smile in the happy silence

so much at one they are
it does not really matter
that their bodies must not touch

PALEONTOLOGY LECTURE: BIRDS (Circa 2500 A.D.)

These balls of frozen feathers shared
The food on which our fathers fared.
But eggs they laid were much too small
To make a human meal at all,
And flesh upon their bones, though sweet,
Was not enough for men to eat.
So since their lives could fit no plan
Envisaged by economic man,
We left them in the wasteland drear
Outside the plastic hemisphere
We raised to hoard the sun's thin gold.
And so these creatures, dead of cold,
Are still preserved. Traditions say
(How true I do not know) that they,
Before they froze on frozen hills,
Made pleasant noises with their bills.

AVALON

I know four girls who might make queens
In timeless Avalon, and they
And I have had our fill of this
Clock-heavy world. But I, alas,
Am neither Arthur nor a king.
Nor is there magic anywhere.

But let's not cry on that account.
Clasp hands, shut eyes to form a ring,
And dance until we all fall down.
Perhaps a dizzy spell will do
What magic can't and in a trice
Swing wide the singing gates of gold.

Out from that burst of vertigo
Which numbs the sense of things that are
We five will sally forth and seize
The dazzling sands that lie between
The orchard bowers of idleness
And the tough, salt-muscled sea.

MAYBASKET KISS

What should I have said to the girl,
Hollow-shanked and skinny-armed
And straight up and down
But with hair like a roan foal?

She covered her face with her hands
But I tore them apart and kissed her
Right on the cheek, and she cried
While I stood and felt like a fool.

What use to plead the occasion and time
Even though it was the first of May?
A girl's first kiss from the boy she loves
Ought not to be taken that way.

A FARMER VIEWS THE HARVEST

The mind's lens on the factual
Turns a dimensional hinge;
Through the flat-surfaced actual
Past and future impinge:

To the retina-reality
Nerves carry each portion
And the telescopic eye
(Fusing distortion)

Reads *coin* for corn-fields dense,
Bread for wheat-ears waving--
Beauty obscured by its consequence,
Life by life's craving.

STATEMENT OF POSITION

Walk not on lonely roads, climb no mountains
To those waste lands of chill and arid air
Where hollow men for lack of other food
Consume themselves until unnatural meals
Being levitation and a giddy head;
Eyes blur bifocal, see two worlds in one,
And in confusion of delirium
Mind takes flesh-hunger for fine food-of-soul.

Flocks throng the valley; here are valley folk
Whose worn paths are shortcuts to quick meeting.
Leading nowhere they lead us together
That each from each may take his natural food,
Reciprocal wine of shared communion
And bread of body's union, broken fast
Of isolation over.

So sustained
Who feeds upon the fruit of lives he feeds
Need never look behind to fear of salt
Nor forward to terror, knowing no drought
Of water, dearth of earthy fare will fret
The man whose journeying need is justified
Not in new road nor record-breaking climb
But by a humbler kind of pilgrimage.

WIND-DANCE

The caught breath draws
now the beautiful
flower, and the jaws
of the grinning skull

close like a knife
and miss their fare,
but the blossom-life
stemmed in swaying air

swings out and in
the narrowing jaws
that wait and grin
for another pause.

PERMANENCE

when white-skulled Winter
rages to draw
blossom and blood
into his maw,

constant to Summer
in hue and form
Art's paper roses
defy his storm

THE FISH OF TIME AND SPACE

Strange fish at night the eye's net gathers in
For there the dart of light that braved the miles
Of emptiness ten thousand years is still
And caught at last in my receptive nerves
With impact lighter than a one-day gnat.

And when I close my lids, they then receive
The nightmare darkness of the one-celled world
That creeps in cold across the galaxies
Of protoplasmic time, and is dissolved
Before the shapes of space that light has made.

WERE YOU TO COME BACK

were you to come back
with fever in your face
and all your flesh
an ache to crave
the healing touch of love

I might not remember
I have no license
to be your physician

FUTILITY

There was a paper man
Who ran a paper mart
And loved a paper love
With all his paper heart.

And when at last he tired
Of leaves instead of life
Into his paper heart
He plunged a paper knife.

THE TRIUMPH OF POETRY

he did
he was
his rest was silence

I did not
I was not
I could not rest

I filled the void
with sounding words

my need-words
found the void in her
moved her from him to me

a Pyrrhic victory

TREE AND BIRD

a blur of hurt
that wrenched my seeds
and blocked the sun
from tender parts
that ached for chlorophyll
you pillaged me

a drop of heavier rain
that bounded erratically
scraping bark and bruising twig
hurting here and there
you woke my dormant cells
to fear and want your touch

now you have gone
this routine stillness
is not pleasant anymore

OF THIS I AM SURE

of this I am sure
that what is etched
by acid act
on heart and brain
will endure
and remain
as fact

and however skilled
an artist
or poet you are
the hues you select
the words you twist
cannot affect
the scar or star

A DEFENCE OF AMATEURISM

I know what the answer is

in all the games I ever played
baseball basketball and golf
I have never been a star

but every honest player shares
the joys the great stars have

occasions when my fielding zeal
pulled off a leaping catch
that lay beyond my skill

the high-arched spin my two hands knew
would cleave the hoop even as it left
my far-extended fingertips

the true faint vibration
that ran along the putter's shaft
to tell my body that the ball
was rolling truly to the cup

these things however rare
were in themselves enough
to justify my efforts and the games

it is that way too with poetry

KORE

Triptolemus, Eumulpus, and Embuleus
Walk sadly down the pasturage of dawn
By that sea-girt Eleusinian meadow
Where a half-pomegranate mocks the corn . . . .

To them it seemed they still might see her
As first they saw her in the April air,
A child who twinkled in a corn-green gown
With scarlet poppies bleeding in her hair.

Triptolemus, Eumulpus, and Embuleus,
Strong violent men whose passions knew no law:
A child less lovely would have been their prey,
But her eyes dissolved their lusts to awe.

Dry wizened grasses glowed beneath her feet,
Her careless touch awoke the sleeping trees,
The sunlight on her kirtle as she moved
Settled like a swarm of golden bees.

Strange light was in the clear sky of those days;
It made the air taste amber wine, and corn
Be food that fed yet left all humgers keen;
Each draught of mead was like a joy new born.

But now the sunlight cannot pierce a thin cloud
And on the frozen meadow hard and chill
Triptolemus, Eumulpus, and Embuleus
Look on the hoofprints of the horse of hell . . . .

133

IN DEFENCE OF ROSARIES

What if I choose
to talk to myself
by finger-touch
on coloured stones?

meanings that my hands
assign their shape and texture
recur more true
than any sound

and God whose stillness
speaks as loud as noise
will understand
my private prayer

and listen to that part
of me which dies
a dumb fish beached
on a sand of words

PREMONITION

somewhere inside the house
a leaking tap
is sealed in silence

a door opens
and the spaced-out drops invade
the rhythm of my dreams

SPIV'S INNISFREE

I will arise and go to a pub in Picadilly
And six quick ones will I down there, of Scotch and
                                  soda made.
A corner seat will I have there, a place where I
                                  can see
The pimps and nancies ply their trade.

And I shall meet a tart there, for tarts go walking
                                  slow,
Walking from New Oxford Street to where th'Embankment
                                  runs;
Where Haymarket's all a-glimmer and Strand a neon glow
They glide for joy of London's sons.

I will arise and go now, for always night and day
I hear soft flesh breathing with low moans in the park--
While I stand on the pavement, or in my bedroom grey,
I hear it in the hot heart's dark.

OVERHEARD IN THE METRO

I

. . . and the man who made
my baby-sitting son cry
by saying things to him about me
that he never dared to say to me
may yet become a dean
before he lives, if ever . . .

II

"No one hates me quite so much
as Julius does."

"What did you do to him?"

"I let him steal my mistress
who then left him of her own accord."

FITNESS

A thrush's voice
by a wind-whipped sea
dwindles to thin
anomaly

while a gull's cry
in a sheltered wood
grates on the sense
an alien mood

now old groves vanish
that sheltered sweet rhyme
cry the gull's cry
this is the gull's time

THE MAN TO WHOM NO ONE LISTENED

at first he adjusted to the change
that slowly crept over him

by shouting till his eardrums ached
he got attention for a while

and then it was with every one
as if he did not speak

but the less that he was listened to
the more it seemed he had to say

without a voice he moved a ghost
through crowds of men and women

who listened with respectful ears
when some one else addressed them

at length it dawned on him
that he might be very sick

an operation then he thought
would sever all his vocal cords

produce in him a cause
at one with consequence

so that he could tell himself
he was different with good reason

but how persuade a surgeon
to take away a non-existent noise

at length he fell into a dream
that nothing could interrupt

in it his voice was mountain-thunder
to the ears of men like frightened mice

who quailed before that mighty sound
and burst their brains and died

TRANSFORMATION

I laid my head at last, my love,
upon your lap
in passion's wood where strange

enchantments are. Then you
grew virginal
in the eyes of my deep care

while underneath the skin
that gentle beast
too long extinct in me,

the boyish unicorn,
awoke and purred
his joy to the unbelieving world.

THE BLACK AND THE GOLD

sheer energy in a skin of form
dances to an ever-being rhythm
in golden rays of shimmering light
against black walls of space and time

something there is akin to light
that drives apart all heaviness
from gravid tug and viscous flow
to curling wave and buoyant air

the breeze that rocks the spider's web
and blows aloft the thistle-seed
is planted in the flow of sap
and in the pulse of driven blood

many rhythms dance the universe;
in light all sex and seasons wave
whose flux contains the teeming life
of time slow-measured by earth's spin

a dance analogous to mind,
that light of self whose nimble thought
through a maze of shifting words must mock
the planet which it warms and feeds

to grasp life's total paradigm
throw wide your window to the night
and watch, to star-tunes echoed here,
gold-shoes beat on a floor of ebony

A LOOK INTO THE FUTURE

like a prospector braving
the desert's drought and wind
in his quest for gold

John Robert Colombo
plods through Hansard
seeking found poems

THE WHORE

he wanted it so much
that when she took his $10.00
the only thing he could do
was hug her on the bed
and cry

- - easy for her, you say

- - I'm not so sure

for a moment
those tears on her breast
almost made her belong
to a profession
even older than
the one she was in

LINES FOR A FIFTY-FOURTH BIRTHDAY

A leg-weary fighter in the thirteenth round
Spars with an opponent he can no longer see
While a voice inside his ears is ringing:
"Keep punching. Keep punching.
You yet can knock him out.
There is still time."

AS LONG AS SHE DOES NOT SAY, I LOVE YOU

As long as she does not say, I love you
you owe her nothing

if you disentangle yourself coolly
she may never say it

and if she does, give her good reasons
why this love is impossible

in that way you will always have her
and you will never be had

remember that time when you first saw
your own mother had rejected you

hurt slammed the door on your heart
so hard it stuck there

THE MAELSTROM

before the act
it was always the same

I made up my mind
to be her instrument
considering her pleasure
above my own

but the impersonal
orgiastic moment
always betrayed me

her individuality
was then so meaningless
that any other woman
would have done as well

though I was glad
when identity was restored
that it was with her
the act had occurred

at first I was ashamed
thinking I had betrayed
all I had heard about love

then I noted that always
her eyes were closed
and I sensed that she too
was lost and alone
in a maelstrom of pleasure

now I know
that for us both
love is not lust
nor its fulfilment
but rather the rising
from drowning
to the safe slow shores
of our outlined selves

no longer alone
in the mutual maelstrom
but human and together

THE CHAINS OF LILIPUTT

It was the chains of Liliputt
Taught Gulliver he was a giant.

TO THOSE WHO SUCCEED IN THIS WORLD

I am a masochist? What is your vice?

PRISMS

All things touching my senses,
These things I receive,
These things I impart,
But with this difference.

All things converge in me,
All things diverge from me,
All things flow through me,
And flowing through me are never the same.

As glass refracts, directing the sunlight,
So I myself refract,
Directing the course of events.

I am a prism through which life pours,
But I am only one of many:
Before they reached and passed through me,
Things perceived, things conceived,
All had flowed through and been twisted
By the interpolation of a million facets.

So that if anything were real in the beginning
Or at any other time,
If anything were original in the beginning
Or at any other time,
They are not so now,
And what they were and are and will be
Is beyond my power of telling . . .

Shifting at different angles
Of refraction through myriad perceptions
And multifold conceptions
Life is pouring through prisms
As Reality becomes Illusion,
As Illusion becomes Reality;
But as the prism shapes and determines
The form and flow of light,
So living becomes purpose and meaning,
Tangible control of an intangible future.

PROS AND CONS

When we wanted the same things at the same times
    the fact that we loved each other doubled
    whatever it was that each of us had
    as the having-joy glowing in us both
    merged with our equal delight in giving

But now whenever she wants something
    at the very time when I do not want it
    or whenever I want something at the wrong time
    or whenever either wants from the other
    what the other does not wish to give

The fact that we love each other
    makes the situation doubly bad

If we were only passing acquaintances
    our differences could be easily passed over

There'd be no reason then for either to give in
    or if one of us put a price on whatever
    it was that he or she wanted from the other
    such a thing would not break like a nightmare
    through the other's dream of love

What we both need is the art of flexibility
    and the knowledge of when to apply it
    so that at the right time we are lovers
    and at the wrong times acquaintances only

Good actors always respond to their cues

But I'd rather stick in the mud
    of a solid misunderstanding than admit
    that what we have is merely an act
    when every nerve in me cries out that it
    is the only thing in this phoney world that is real

A DREAM IN TWO PHASES

I

A red-blood moon low-hangs the wood
where frosted stubble joins
the bony dance of unfrocked trees

Wind falls. A fantastic dwarf
leers up between the open field and me

Grey-naked over bone in silver light
with teeth that gnash yet make no noise
it casts no shadow on the moonlit sward

We eye each other in the sudden cold
a cat-leap, a grey hand grips my hand
and hot electric power comes from it
creeping up along my arm

I thrill with joy and horror
as I know that when that current hits
my heart, my heart will cease to beat

I stir and pulse inside myself
reversing with surprising ease
that creature's puny flow

beyond my hand and up its arm
to touch the heart I drive
I am alone beneath the moon

But the oneness that I felt
When our two currents joined
is with me still. I feel fulfilled.

II

A red-blood moon low-hangs the wood
of cypress trees inside the cemetery

Wind falls. A fantastic dwarf
leers up beside a nearby tombstone

Grey-naked over bone in silver light
with teeth that gnash yet make no noise
it casts no shadow on the grass

We eye each other. It is sudden warm,
I cross to it: "My brother ghoul,
how would you like to lunch with me,
A new-dead baby ought to do for two."

We merge: the red moon pales
before the radiance of a face.
I hear a whisper somewhere in myself
It's been so long and cold alone.

THE GOLDEN LURE

An epicure will watch with glee
a dying fish, and thrill to know
what living colours ebb and flow
from a heart that bursts in agony.

Like him, your appetite is art
where passion makes a daintier dish
each time, as in that rainbow fish,
it blazes from a broken heart.

So when, a golden lure, you break
the liquid surface of my eye,
the foolish fish of joy awake
then dart beneath to safety.

For there's one truth I've learned holds good
That the merely loved can never share:
Whoever drowns in water would
Not wish a fish to drown in air.

THE ANTIDOTE

He found them bobbing from adjacent branches
of an alder bush, just above the snow-line

and he knew from the moth-book's illustration
just what they were, two cocoons of *telea polyphemus,*
each a thumb of silk with alder leaves adhering

he took them to his cellar and he kept them
in a shoe box with slits on top and sides
to give them air for wintering

every day in Spring he raised the cover
and peeked inside and saw no change at all

then one afternoon in early June
he noted that a cocoon had its end removed
and in the far dark corner of the box
a bloated travesty was stirring

it trailed a huge and slimy belly
along the cardboard floor and fanned
the stumps of wings whose flabby veins
had not hardened into form and colour

out of the other cocoon's smaller end
there came two antenna plumes; their vibrations
made a blur that contradicted
their owner's slow emerging girth

once free, that moth's vibrations caught
the other's, and in a flash
ungainly bulk crossed space and bodies joined

Just then his mother called. He put the lid
back on the box and went to her.
When he came back, it was not the same.

He swept aside the lid. Both moths were dead,
their undeveloped wings bent in shreds. their
                              bodies unabsorbed,
and the box was strewn with eggs that looked
for all the world like flattened pills.

And always after that there came to him
the memory of a leap,
of bodies blurring into one,

and somewhere in him then a pattern formed

A LOVE LETTER

We met like leaves that touched and clung before
The wind's whim swept them from the air:
Now from the warmth that joining brought to both
One memory is all we share.

Nor should we try to keep in mind its shape
Against time's ruthless, slow decay,
Nor fresh embalm in words, as poets do,
The radiant corpse of yesterday.

The ink with which I write this letter dries
Before my thoughts are out of sight.
Only a mind more lead than yours would prize
The cold, stiff words a pen can write;

For neither thought nor word can quite preserve
The blood of joy, nor can they keep
Alive the ghosts of possibility
When quick with life the futures leap.

Therefore in this, our winter solstice, love,
Let us not vex our souls with strife
But rather wait the wind that cannot fail
To bring again the touch of life.

CLAIRE

An ugly, inward child
    coltish, long-limbed, long-faced
    with flesh unrounded over bone,

Claire would twist and grimace
    as if naked on the stage
    beneath unwinking stares

Whatever eyes looked at her
    became glint-steel binoculars
    her own eyes in the mirror were the same

Came the magic year of change
    no one enjoyed her metamorphosis
    from gawk to beauty more than Claire

Who belled at nightly balls and swept
    from beaux to beaux in triumph,
    living to exhaustion's utter edge

As if she dreaded -- as she did --
    the beetle-dream that gripped her still
    the one where boys bent sun-rays

Magnified through giant glass-shards
    that cracked and burnt her shell
    and as she feebly dodged them

She heard loud laughter ringing
    sharper, shriller, till it blended
    with the agony of light

THE HUNTSMEN

Into the woods in Autumn
A myriad huntsmen trail
To lull their blood's misgivings
Through slaughter of the frail;

For all the deer they gaze on
Once more in them awake
Pale ghosts of useless beauty
That must die for manhood's sake;

Forbidden flowers of women
Whose thorns can pierce a skull
Where neither wives nor duty
May nullify nor pull . . .

They squeeze their triggers madly
And blast the does to bits,
And part of them is shattered
Each time a bullet hits.

WORD-GAME

casual
    as a stone
        a word
whips waves
    in mind-sea
that die
    when it sinks

star
    a fire-hole
        centred
cracks
    rays outward
        fishlines
in the dark
    reverse inward
and catch
    star

star-fish
　　　　　star shrinks
plunges
　　　　　huddles in ooze
casual
　　　like a stone

why do words
　　　　　　come
where do they
　　　　　go
where are they
　　　　　　when
they are not

THE HOUSE WITHOUT A DOOR

If only I knew where it was
so I could say yes to it
as I have said yes to so many things
that fizzled or in this dimension
shaped and fed the upright citizen
the comfortable acquaintance
the easy friend
and kept in neat repair
the house in which I live

If only I knew where it was
I would not need these dreams

When night unshapes all rooms
something comes to life
in the grim glee of violated taboos
and rejoices most of all
as its naked turpitude
is shockingly exposed

150

The unshaped thing that grows in darkness
is more living than the life
my daylight knows

If only I knew where to find it
I would reach that doorway
turn myself the key
unlock the dark
and set it free
as light
a quivering
acopalypse of being

But it is lost somewhere, I know
in the house that Jack built
out of his non-needs for show
a house too crammed to fit him
till he stunted his real needs
to live in it so

nothing less than a bomb, I fear
will raze it now
and let him grow

TRIPLE MEETING

Three strangers on this page --
tree, you, and I --
as one converge to light
a flame of joy:

this paper and these words
are cold and dead;
the match that makes them blaze
is in your head.

BURT

burnt-out and done at forty
his war-wound complicated by T.B.
and the waste of over-work and too much play
Burt could no longer hope to hold a job

and so he sat in front of Simpson's store
and earned a constant cigarette
by entertaining all the local lads
with lurid tales of World War I
the only time in all his life
men treated him as though he were a man

unless you count those brief mad days
when he drove his brand-new
horse-and-buggy through the quiet streets
lighting his cigarettes with dollar-bills
--a six-months' wonder of the rural world—
until his army-severance pay was gone

". . . we used to line up Jerry prisoners
and turn their own guns on them
to see how many a Mauser bullet
could go through.
The count was always just the same,
two men's bodies and about half a third."

(His eyes lit up a moment
just before he shuddered through a cough)
"I tell you, boys, those were the days.
A man with a gun was god."

AS NAKED NOW AS EVER

As naked now as ever
Cupid hunts with bow and quiver,
And bags more human game
Than the guns of Mars can claim.

UNHAPPY CLOWN

Where are your tears, unhappy clown?
Where are your tears?
--Alone in the night
When no one's in sight
And my heart the burden bears,
There are my tears.

Why smile you now, unhappy clown?
Why smile you now?
--I smile and I sing,
And I laugh like a king
For the same reason as you,
To be part of the show.

THE EVENT

   *   *   *   *

To describe it would only feed
the appetites of dung-flies.

In itself an event is nothing.
It dies in the acting.

But its ghost walks and rocks
the minds of all it touches
as a stone vibrates in water
rippling far and thin
to the shores of time.

   *   *   *   *

There were four involved:
Rory, Sam, Arthur, and Bella.

   *   *   *   *

To Rory, remembering,
there was relish
in his brute breaking of her.

Fear in her rabbit eyes
woke a cold-snake malevolence
of will,
induced a hunger in him
not even the last great war
could satiate,
and ended him at Ortona
when at exactly the wrong time
blood-lust blotted out caution.

   *   *   *   *

No, no, Sam. Don't hurt me, Sam!

Sound-waves soon dissolve
and become inaudible at sixty yards.

But still now and then
their tapes re-run across his brain
impulses that score indelibly
the velvet soil of self-esteem
so that pride in children, wife,
and all his good deeds done
can hardly hide the gashes
that they make, tilling
his self to harvest humbleness of love.

   *   *   *   *

Arthur blamed himself the most
for having told the other boys
just where it was that he had seen
the feeble-minded Bella
in a clearing back behind
the Woodson's old abandoned house,
dancing her moonlit dance
and aping in a clumsy-legged way
some movie actress she remembered.

Technically he had not done a thing.
He had only stood on guard and watched
the boys doing what they did
after they cornered her.

The girl's an idiot. What happened there
could not have mattered in her life.

This truth meant just as much to him
as knowing Christ was God had meant
to Judas on the night he hanged himself,
and in that dark all moral colours blurred
he beamed a midnight round him till he die

   * * * *

In her own dead-end world of feeling
the event to Bella was a light
of fear and pain, as a red-light signal
gets to be to any one
after a zooming cab
has struck him down.

It did not really hurt her much;
just enough to make quite sure
she never danced again.

   * * * *

Events are ghosts that walk and make us move.
This was only one.

   * * * *

What if the myriads moving through
each one of several billion lives
clash and jostle as this one did,
tangling us in a bloody web
till we have neither sight to see
nor strength to fly?

   * * * *

The spider-god of history
thrives on ghosts

"IN WILDNESS IS THE PRESERVATION OF THE WORLD."

. . . that Spring evening
along a rutted road
by old McNally Ferry
our car bumped to a halt
under the young maples
and we listened to the birds
go crazy in their joy
until our hands and lips and flesh
were rhythmic birds that moved
in soundless rhythms of their own

ten years later
I navigated the river's murk
above the dam
and dived to find tree-skeletons
with naked limbs — where darting fish
and blobs of mud suggested birds

for New Brunswick's good
men built that dam
and changed the river's contours
and there is room
for trees to grow for birds to sing
somewhere else

we, too, built dams for others' good
and changed our feelings' contours
and there are hands and lips and flesh
no doubt can move and sing with ours
somewhere else

all the same it is not the same

THE BEST OF TIMES

After the chores were over
and the dishes put away
we used to sit together
in the kitchen
and listen to the rain
whose coolness blessed
our tired bodies
and our planted fields

There was nothing to do

nothing to want

and nothing to talk about

OVERHEARD IN THE METRO: III

". . . my dreams I enjoyed
until I read Freud. . ."

POET

he wove a cloak of words to wear
against the constant pull
of water, fire, earth, and air
that bruised his will

he drew the coat he made quite fast
on skin and eyes and mouth
till words were all the sense that passed
his brain as truth

what can he weave with now for cloak
against the constant pull
of elemental words that shake
and bruise his will?

157

JIM ROWAN

A beggar stopped us in the street.
Jim Rowan turned his pockets out:
"It's only money, lad," he said,
"And there's lots of that about."

That day Jim missed a vital putt
And smiled to see what he had done:
"It's just a game, my boy," he said,
"Tomorrow who will care who won."

And later in the bar he left
A lass he could have had to me:
"There'll be other nights for love," he said,
"And other girls as good as she."

But though a prince, Jim Rowan moves
And takes or leaves what comes with grace
I'll not trade my hope or agony
To stand at ease in Rowan's place.

THE END OF POETRY

Forever always is the Word
and the Word is servant unto men
so that whatsoever a man utters
that will be.

In the morning of the world
the first poet saw the first woman

"Your eyes," he said, "are emeralds . . ."
(as he spoke she was stricken blind)

". . . and your lips are ripe red plums."
(she screamed as squishing juice
ran sweetly down her chin.)

The poet saw and fled
to a universe
of less rigorous reality
where still his children sing.

PROGRESS

in the beginning
naked hunger
soaked in a brine of food

the brine grew thin
uncertain in its whereabouts

and some cells multiplied
combined to mobile units

and overlaid each self
with sex and sense

to feed their hunger
and to hide their nakedness

now they know they are
that did not know

what else has changed

CLASSROOM

a great gust of words
bends our student heads to one
attentive level

in the yard outside
each flower shapes itself in the
silence of the sun

PAPER ROSES

Now white-skulled Winter
rages to grind
blossom and blood
out of the mind

constant to Summer
in hue and form
these paper roses
defy his storm.

A CLASSICIST'S LAMENT

Though once a slave before tradition's throne,
The poet now need please himself alone.
No more by patient toil, as Horace schools,
He serves a stern apprenticeship to rules.
A youth, new bitten by the flea to write,
Can scratch himself to poet overnight!
Pebbles that lurk beneath the self's dark sea
Can win acclaim as pearls of poetry,
Provided that the ropes on which they're strung
Are twisted dreams by Freud or myths by Jung;
For, like high priests whose revenue depends
Upon a lore no layman comprehends,
The modern critic gives his best reviews
To work that's esoteric and abstruse,
And should it prove too dense (like courtier bold
Who praised the king's new clothes in fable old)
Boldly he'll vaunt the poem's well-cut shape
And trace rich patterns where the public gape . . .

Oh, for an honest child to cry halloo
For naked truths that Burke and Johnson knew,
Or another Pope from Twickenham
To drop clean acid from a poisoned pen.

THE DAY

When she met him at the airport
both had much to say but said little
not knowing how properly to begin

He who had been bold in his thoughts
while awaiting this moment
was now in the proximity of her flesh
too uncertain shy to speak the words
lest what he said might startle her

During the long circuitous ride to her home
she punctuated the silence
with comments on the scenery
drawing his eyes to what had gone unnoticed
were it not for her quiet constant gift
of noting beauty in the dust of routine things

She gave him breakfast in the kitchen
and with it served champagne
till they slipped into a pitch and toss of phrase
as graceful and unconscious as two players
playing catch to warm up arms
just before a game begins

The house, she said, was only rented
but he could see that every room
in colour tones and unobtrusive grace
became an extension of herself
and as they wandered through the house
their words half-opened guarded doors

She told him of her two sons, and how
their natures meshed or jarred
and what their leaving meant to her

He talked to her about his boys
but could not bring himself
to speak about his wife
and she kept still about her husband

Late afternoon the sun set in the park
with water, geese, and autumn's shredded leaves
all softened to a glory in the dying light
her face, he saw, had altered
to a girl's young face the while her eyes
drank in the cider moment to its lees
and he felt chaste and humbled by her happiness

After the pleasant dinner and the wine
they sat in chairs beside the fireplace
watching the struggling flames

 She told him how, a little girl,
she'd slipped into her grandfather's room
and how that dying man had gripped her shoulder
so that ever after such a touch restored
that moment to her being in all its sharpness
grief inexpressible

And as he listened, in the embers
a blaze of honour came alive
washing their brows with so intense a light
that all lust shadows faded from their flesh
and they were simple children then
who knew their game of love could only be
a game of make believe
but loved each other none the less for that

And after that he talked a little too
about his worries and his weariness
taking her sympathy as a birthday present
his by right but welcome all the same

There was in him a story
just as meaningful and intimate
as hers about her grandfather
but through long habit of defense
he did not leave himself so vulnerable
as tell it her -- afterwards he wished he had
but hoped she would not notice
this particular lack in him

She drove him to the plane
in silence that was warm and comfortable
a garment to hold in and shield
the tender edges of that day

At the airport their short kiss
to each was *Ita, Missa Est,*
the then conclusion of a sacrament.

CRUELTY

He crawled on his belly to me
As I have crawled before fate,
And his brown eyes' humility
Mirrored the weak life I hate.

The day had gone hard with me,
And my hand held a log . . .
How can I tell the jury
I struck at myself, not the dog?

POETESS

as a house-wife
wipes and puts back
her falling china
when earthquakes crack

she rubs up thoughts
until each shines
then sets them down
in even lines

for no fond hope
of ills withstood
but just because
it does her good

THE CRYSTAL MOMENT

for the passing of desire, do not mourn;
it like a rainbow is perpetually reborn

but oh, the crystal moment which you took,
that shaped and held the flame before it broke

its shards lie shattered on a dusty shelf
deep in the cluttered store-room of your self

A MORAL DILEMMA

I wish I were a pig
when pearls are scattered
on the ground before me

then I wouldn't have to
answer questions:

"How can I get the mud off them
without it rubbing off on me?"

Or if there isn't any mud
look for further answers:

"Am I fit that such etherial radiance
should touch these hands?"

"Are they lost, and will their owner
come and claim them from me?"

"Can I keep them clean and shining
in the places where I go?"

I wish I were a pig
when pearls are scattered
on the earth before me

All I'd have to do
is eat, digest them,
make them part of pig

end all problems and all pearls

A PRAYER

O You, whose loving laws designed
The knots that men and women hold,
Lord of the hearth and home, be kind
To all who chafe in bands of gold - -

Poor fools who walk staid roads and crave
The high, bird-travelled sky above,
Who want the things they dare not have
And have the things they will not love.

TENSION

If it ticked to the tense of the spring of my heart
The clock of my life would go mad as I hold you,
And time would unwind in a spinning blur
That ended the need of us both for all time;
But the little smooth wheels of propriety mesh
To check in its course my mainspring's motion
Till it slows to the tick of a prudent release
That is timed to the sway of your hairspring passion
As the great spring of love is held in and bent,
Tormented by tension that waits between ticks.

ART

Light bird of life
your death is sealed
even as we glimpse
the form revealed:

Strong though you soar,
marble, notes, words
kill the brave flight
with static swords.

PENELOPE

Three loves had Penelope
And two were flesh to her,
But a man who died full long ago
Became her one master.

Her first love was a farmer
Who kept her snug and warm
But treated her like any chattel
He cared for on his farm.

She left him for a sailor,
A free and easy man,
Till a seagull sat upon the window.
The next day he was gone.

She heard a priest proclaiming:
"No man can make you whole.
You will never rest till Jesus
Is the great love of your soul."

Now she is Jesus' chattel,
A sailor, too, is He,
For He loves to net the soul-fish
In the meshes of eternity.

But she keeps the net quite meekly
No matter how men call,
For He has left His bleeding heart
In a picture on her wall.

And He set her fingers working,
Weaving heaven by His word,
Ave, Maria, plena gratia,
Faithful to her king and lord.

HOW SIMPLE SIMON PUT THE KIBOSH ON THE DEVIL

Sim thinks he's a roaring lion
or a winged dragon maybe
with fangs and claws to sieze and tear

And to Hepsibah
he's a hooded snake
that lurks to bruise her naked heel

George saw him in a movie once
a glib-tongued gentleman
like a parson or a city dude

They laugh at what I tell them
a dream, they say, is all you had
and it has scared away your wits

But the three of them are wrong
for the devil came to me
and we had it out all right

By the time we'd finished and I'd put
the kibosh on him good and well
I knew him as I knew myself

He had a lot of nerve to come the way he did
to my room at evening after church
and me, a Christian almost from my birth

Imagine if you can a naked girl
as lovely as a movie queen
but except for sex my living twin

*   *   *   *

To touch your own flesh is an empty thing
unless your mind can shape a woman
and feed itself on that

To touch a woman's flesh's a chancy thing
another rhythm that you can't blot out
competes too strongly with your own

This rhythm was a rhythm-twin
my self was moving with a woman self
as touch-to-feel and feel-to-touch were one

*   *   *   *

I was lost and done for then
had I not raised my head
where moonlight on a mirror gleamed

and showed me, lying on my bed,
a teen-aged boy threading his rosary
as his left hand gripped a crucifix

The flesh beside me felt rough and cold
a stranger's eyes glared straight at mine
and my left hand gripped a club

I swung it and I swung and swung
and every blow caved in the skull
that grew again as fast as it was hit

and my own brain ached and throbbed
as the pain transferred to me
and my arms grew numb from pounding

I dared not stop, for if I did
before the darkness stopped
the fiend would have me

At last a wan sun caught me
feebly pounding at a pillow,
blank and white beside me, with a crucifix

                *   *   *   *

I, Simon, now am empty of all evil
having beat the old scratch out of me
whatever Sim or George or Hepsibah may say

Even though I let him in through weakness
I put the kibosh on him all the same
and I'm pretty sure he'll not come back

with my trusty crucifix I did it
thanks to You, O Lord, Who let me see
the purest prayer I ever prayed

But come back, Lord, and pour Your Grace
in every pore that's clean for you
Nothing else can fill this emptiness

THE THING MAY MET

the thing May met was
real all right and certainly
no unicorn

it shredded her young
girl's dream like a bridal gown
caught on a bull's horn

COOLIE

up the slow hill-road
Li struggles as shade trees grow
cooler for his load

LIMBO

in memory's tomb
the bones of my past
lie dusty and still

re-membered reshaped
and resurrected
as the glorious body
of an immortal poem
that still might live

but the christ of art
withholds his hand

did the life
that these were
consume his energy

or does he fear the pain
of another crucifixion

TIME'S CONJURER

After he looked at the large
    wall-mirror
             he realized
he'd be bigger
         in a smaller room
And the naked bulb-light
    on those wrinkles
             told him
he'd look younger
         in a dimmer light
He knew that with a tortoise
    for a pet

       the way he walked
would also seem
       quite fast

Time's conjurer
    his tricks
       with space and light
so formed a permanent
         illusion

that to all who saw him
    still life
       became still death
indistinguishably
       the same

PROGRESS

Rude Ixion,
the father blind,
a goddess divined
in a cloud at dawn

and died for reward
as mist turned woman --
joy more than human
brain-stabbed by fear's sword.

His son (who for years
had hardened his brain
with facts in a chain
too tight-linked for fears)

swivelled a proud
telescopic eye
over the sky
and found only cloud.

TAO

Five players in an endless game
That move together to one end --
Charm, Zest, Rhythm, Grace, and Glame --

They wind inside and out a frame
Of matter which our senses tend,
Five players in an endless game.

Charm is a pool of waters tame
Where reeds of Grace may smoothly bend
To winds whose morning breath is Glame

On Rhythm of the sunlight's flame,
With Zest the magic of the blend.
Five players in an endless game

That move as one: Life, Way, and Name
of God, the Source alike and End:
Charm, Zest, Rhythm, Grace, and Glame.

--So sang Lao Tze, who saw the same
And in one brush-stroked sign did blend
Charm, Zest, Rhythm, Grace, and Glame,
Five players in an endless game.

THE TUNNEL

he had been moving along it
longer than he could remember

it hadn't seemed so bad at first

there had been crowds with him then
and it had either been downhill
or on the level at least

people could talk and sing together
share in the wayside fruit
or rest together on the beds provided

and always it seemed in those days
that maybe around the next turning
a door would lead out of the tunnel
into a pleasant garden

at any rate there had been windows
that let in light on himself
and on all his fellows
making them sparkle with beauty

now the crowd had lost its magic
he could hardly hear the songs
windows were few and far apart
their dim light quenched in the chill air

uphill now he plodded on
stumbling over mere pebbles
slept fitfully on cold beds
kept his mind on earlier stages
tried not to notice narrowing walls
blackness that gathered
to a point just ahead

QUESTION

without ceasing to be me
I can be the bird I see
there on the spray
in every feather he
though in my own way

but where's the guarantee
that I am not some dim
creature in that bird's whim
that makes me be the me
that looks at him?

LEAVES AND THE WIND

The wind that stirs the leaves is sharp and cold.
The yellow leaves are dead. But in my heart
Their rustling sound awakes the restless ghost
Of one who walked with hair of beech-tree gold
Beneath live leaves.

                   It is as if a wind
Of autumn mind blew through my brain
And in the gathered leaf-mould of the years
Turned up one leaf still green despite all frost.

THE LEAF

Think of that green and twisted leaf
One autumn day caught in her hair
When at the last to save herself
She left you standing where you were

Unfaded through the years it is
And green in every curving vein
When all your memories of bliss
Have blurred and left your brain

Take crayon, paper, draw it now
As it still lives inside your head
Then let me see. I want to know
What lasts to live when love is fled.

THE TREE

Its roots are hands to scoop up rain
its leaves are throats that drink the sun
these disappear when warmth is done
the whole tree is the whole tree's brain

and every scar it has will heal
no matter where the wound may be
but anywhere upon the tree
too great a scar will slowly kill

without lungs it breathes but has no breath
without a heart its thin blood flows
with no eyes it light and darkness knows
and it knows too of coming death

for feeling in its wounded cells
will cause a crippled tree to fling
more blossoms to the winds of spring
than one whom youthful sap impels

IN A HOSPITAL

in a hospital
a breath of infant breath blends
with a last-gasp death

the child does not know
he is alive nor the man
that his breathing's done

nor can those watchers
who pronounce that one is dead
and the other born

say with certainty
of what they saw before them
any more than this

"in a hospital
we watched two breaths meet in time
the rest in silence"

MOTION IS MEANING

motion is meaning
a forming that slips
into and out of
a shapeless dark

when from everything
each sorting being
hardens to shape
each various Now

bright patterns glow
trapped on time's string
as the frail beads flash
air threaded on bone

AGAINST PERSPECTIVE

Watch that man
on the runway there
He dwindles as your plane
noses upper air
and vanishes even
as you scan

Time, too,
is such a plane
What space can do
time can as well
even to me
even to you

Time and space
are false compasses
and kill all hope
Art is the true pole
in a kaleidoscope
Art lies within

Watch that man
then close your eyes
and keep them closed
until your plane
has reached the skies
He will not disappear

Then draw his face
each telling line
in due proportion
and in proper place
You may have cheated time
as you have cheated space

THE REED

"Man is a thinking reed."
—Blaise Pascal.

clear and cool the reed
stood lordly tall, proud and calm
in yet unstirred air

as I moved my lungs
the same reed danced and trembled
courtier to my breath

when my weight of need
fell on it, the reed made one
with hard, wounding earth

when I rose it rose,
straight and stiff as if no storm
had ever touched it

from which I know now
the hollow hearts we rule are
mere superior grass

AN EVENING WITH EMILY

In the raw damp air the street was a long sewer lined with lights — regular rows of street lamps and intermittent blurred squares of windows. At last I found the number and pressed the button.

The voice of one at once fulfilled and relaxed with age: "Emily isn't in yet, and it's very late. Perhaps you had better come back tomorrow."

"I've come too far not to see her. May I wait?"

A hesitation. "Yes, come in." The mask of an old woman looked at me.

My knees bent, and I sank into the comforting softness of an armchair; pink, it was in the dim light, and somehow enveloping — like an overripe tomato. Across from me was the window facing the street and framing the blurred bars of light from a Venetian blind across the way.

At my elbow, out of a middle-aged mask, the voice of a woman spoke — neither fulfilled nor relaxed. "Milk or lemon?" This must be Emily's sister. The other, I knew, was her aunt.

A cup of tea materialized on the table by my elbow. Slowly I sipped and closed my eyes from fatigue. Out of the drifting darkness faintly the words came to me:

"It's like Emily to keep us waiting up like this."

"You mustn't blame her. After all, her mother died when she was only ten and her father has let her do anything she has liked ever since."

Silence. Then, sharp with tension, the unfulfilled voice:

"It isn't that. It's that man. He's here again. It's his pretty face and his hate that keep Emily from us."

Were they talking about me? I hadn't a pretty face. I opened my eyes to semi-darkness, then adjusted them carefully to light; for there on the wall to the left of the window, shining and white was 'him'. He was no mask, but a human face — the face of a young man, wide-eyed and tortured with emotion over a naked bust that seemed suspended in air, though next to it and beneath it glimmered the shadowy suggestion of arms, legs, and torso.

"Who are you?" he said. I shivered. Where had I seen that face before? Where had I heard that voice?

"I'm a friend of Emily —"

"You lie!" he screamed. "Emily has no friend but me!" — and he rushed at me.

I caught him in my arms, and he jerked me out of the chair. We rolled on the floor together toward a lighter patch in the room. His strength was more nervous than muscular, and I easily mastered him. He broke into sobs:

"I wish I were dead. I wish I were dead. Everybody hates me, and I hate myself. I hate what I am."

"You don't have to hate what you are," I said. "If you don't like what you are, you can always be different."

"Can I really be somebody else?"

"Yes, if you want to enough. You can be whatever you want to be."

"Oh, I love you for that," he said, and put both hands on my shoulders, bringing his face close to mine. "Kiss me, kiss me."

And as his face drew nearer me, I saw in the growing light that his hair had burst over his shoulders in glossy waves of black, that his eyes were very large and very blue, that his face had become softer and finer-featured, and that his thin breasts were no longer the breasts of a man but the breasts of a woman. Stranger still was what lay below those breasts. The flesh outlines of a woman's torso were complete, though all the centre was a concave shadow where, it seemed to me, it ought to have been convex. I pushed her away from me.

"You are not Emily."

"Yes," she said, "I am your Emily."

*   *   *   *   *

The crowd was gathering in knots on the edge of the lake below the mill. As I strode rapidly through the rain, I heard angry voices. "Drowned him —" "I bet that witch Emily had something to do with it." "We'll make her pay —"

The voices dwindled, and I was alone in moonlight as bright as day — the rain's aftermath — in the grassy declivity where the giant iron sewer that carries the lake water under the road ends in the gardens of the great mansion. And there, lying on the grass, was Emily, water and mud matting her hair into shaky coils and mottling the ivory whiteness of her limbs — water and mud mingled with touches of some darker substance that could conceivably have been blood. But the eviscerated hollow that was all she was from her breast to her groin gleamed rosy red interspersed with darker lines set in geometric patterns. Quickly she drew me down beside her in the grass.

"You don't think I'm a murderer, do you?" she panted. "You believe in me no matter what you see and what they say."

"Yes," I said, "I believe in you, no matter what I see or what they say."

"I love you," She pulled me to her. Suddenly I felt myself engulfed in a soft pliable body that folded round and over me like the moist folds of a giant vagina. Startled, I recoiled. At this moment, a voice came sharp and clear behind her.

"Emily."

"Yes, father."

"You naughty girl."

She struggled to her feet and stood, head hanging like a crest-fallen child, and suddenly became slimmer as though her outer body were contracting in a pitiful attempt to hide the nakedness of her hollow viscera.

"Come with me. You must take your punishment this time."

Like a whipped dog, she slunk away after her father toward the half-roofed shed at the foot of the cliff.

*   *   *   *   *

Inside the great house we sat down, each silent in his appointed place. Costly dishes gleamed in candlelight. At the head of the table sat Emily's father, calm as a Roman emperor against the din outside.

"We do not begin," he said, "until Emily arrives."

Outside the intermittent mutter of the mob became a blurred ominous shouting. There came the sound of rocks crashing from a height.

"They are stoning the shed," I cried. "Will no one move?" No one moved.

I could stand it no longer. I rushed from the table, out the door, into the open. At the cliff's edge, men and women were concentrating upon hurling large and small stones over the cliff to overwhelm the old tool shed.

"Two can play at that game," I said.

One by one I picked up the frenzied men and women and threw them over the cliff. As they landed upon the hard stones which they had just heaved over, the spirit of their madness changed and they became a search party, flinging aside the stones and clearing away the rubble in a desperate attempt to find Emily. I rushed to join them.

We found her finally, at the bottom of the water tank. Tenderly we extricated her and laid her upon the splintered floor. Her eyes were closed, her skin was death-grey, and her visceral hollow was livid and raw as a piece of meat on a butcher's slab.

I felt a hand touch my shoulder. I turned, and there stood her father, naked and no longer majestic, but grinning and pointing his finger at the spot where his daughter lay.

"Get that grin off your face, you murderer!" I snapped. "You had better make yourself scarce or this mob will stone you to death."

There was something so ludicrous in the naked speed of his bow-legged retreat that I dissolved into uncontrollable laughter.

When I came to myself, the crowd had gone, and Emily stood naked and upright in the moonlight. The geometrical pattern and the hollow shell that had been her body beneath her breasts had disappeared and in their place was true, well-proportioned flesh. She was now as completely woman as any woman could be.

I spoke to her, but she neither saw nor heard me. She turned from me into the arms of a man who had walked through the broken window toward her. Handsome he was, and young — but his face as he winked at me was the face of her father come again. As their bodies were lost into each other, I saw surrounding them both, thin bars of light like the bars of a golden cage. Then nothing.

*　　*　　*　　*　　*

"They've just snapped out the light across the way." Plaintive and weary, the unfulfilled voice filled up the vacuum. *"Emily still isn't home. Maybe she won't be coming home tonight. If we only had a place to put you —"*

*　　*　　*　　*　　*

I walked down the street. The houses were dark and the rain-filled evening had given way to full moonlight. The stars were high and far in a milky sky, but the lamps that lined the street were as regular as the gold bars of a cage. I moved into the centre of the street and walked, looking neither to the right nor to the left.

EPIPHANY

when each leaf and twig
each bird and flower
mud grass and sky
are a flood tide
of living light
and the merged light
of the separate suns
that all things are
pours from the core
of all their being
and floats in air
flaming like white wine
with its own radiance

I receive
and am that light
am each leaf and twig
each bird and flower
mud grass and sky
with no skin between
as the light I am
the wine-sun of me
sparkles and merges
with existence
more keen and real
in the vital flood
than when inside

then the light ebbs
the inner essence
of what each is
shrinks to its source

and the temporal sun
with its squint beams
lights only difference
in each twig and leaf
each flower and bird

sky grass and mud
I and all these
caught held and bound
in separate skins

PARADOX

When I was small
I gazed at the sun
and the light grew black

and when I missed
a tackle and crashed
a fence with my head
that darkness blazed with suns

I remember, too,
the clarity and volume
of our radio
before the overload
blew out the tubes
when I
connected it wrong

Out of these memories
arose my soul's belief
that I died in my birth
that I shall live in my death
and that in eternity
both life and death are one

What wonder then
that I need so many things
to make me forget
this hollowness
of half-existance
that we call life?

MIRACLE

. . . that a love like ours
so late begun
should fly above age and fear

be a mating of eagles
that quiver with sun
high in the stainless air

HIGH-RISE, CANAL, AND CARILLON

high-rise and dark canal
have made the roads that lead to you
smooth ways all men and cars must take
heroics have no place

the carillon chimes
and you are painfully aware
of time, a non-existent thing
that moves unwilling lives

o you, a high-rise princess
and I, a would-be hero, caught
in toils of concrete things like thoughts
whose shapes are trapped in stone

unthink all thought unthink
all being but this now and let
the walls we two together rear
keep Ottawa at bay

what though it may not last
a timeless moment's afterglow
has power to turn canal, carillon
and high-rise into gold

AT THE RECEPTION

for P. K. Page

Alone, he could be
with them
in the most suitable way,
eliding all unpleasantness
and blank routine,
enlarging intimacies,
subtly shifting
nuances, making
memory coincide
with dreams.

Yes, he could live
with people
in his mind,
keeping loneliness at bay.

But in the crowded room
their voices, manners
jostled him
with the difference
between what they were
and what their image
as he held it was.

And it came to him
that he and all the others
were but shards
of a unique vase,
a fragile possibility
that shattered
as the tenuous dreams
of each exploded
through the hubbub of the throng.

HOMAGE

words are merely words, made out of black letters
lines are only lines, however they may run

and this page on which I draw or write
is never more than two-dimensional

whether good or bad my skill
beyond its flatness is illusion

whatever it may impart of you
all art is beaten by your beauty

for that in you is no illusion
nor is it held by lines and words

oh every moment in your being
is replete with four dimensions

let this poem, defeated small
pay you homage, queen

AT THE MID-POINT OF THE MOON'S ECLIPSE

At the mid-point of the moon's eclipse
for one shimmering instant
shadow and light changed places
in an impossible mating
of bright and dark

and to this day I do not know
whether that miracle occurred
somewhere beyond the skies
or in my eyes' nerve-ends
because I wanted it to be
and you were there

TO OTHERS ONLY BECAUSE

he is an interesting man
to others only because
he is interested in a subject
which in turn is interesting
to others only because
he is an interesting man

FLIES ON ICE

before cold came they were
wing-glints in sun-air
slim self-driven darts
that only life imparts
with hunger in their breath
and nectar-sipping tongues

now frozen by a glacier's lungs
their inert forms proclaim
the still-life nothingness of death
vacuity of time

THANKS TO YOU

I have never won
a million dollars in a lottery
but thanks to you, my darling,
I know exactly
what the winner meant
when he said in an interview:
"I'm through gambling for life.
What could I possibly win
more than I have already?"

REFLECTIONS ON READING MARION ENGEL'S *BEAR*

in this case
I do not have
the right academic reactions

is it on my part
a matter of tongue-envy?

or is it rather
the horror of a foreseeable
literary bestiary
in Canada
where only man is vile?

in our fictional stock-exchange
will *Bear* be followed by *Bull*?

or will our great tradition
merely culminate in *Beaver*?

WHAT EVERY CHILD KNOWS ABOUT NOTICE

a few can attract all eyes
just by being themselves

some try to work or run
impress by what they're doing

others take to building
what they make may be noticed

but there's an easier way
the rank-and-file discover

any one who destroys
will receive instant attention

THE PIPES OF PAN

The pipes of Pan were pleading,
"Come, dance with me away!"
And my wayward heart was heeding
The pipes of Pan that day.

I met a maid, a farmer's daughter.
She laughed at me and ran,
But in the meadow there I caught her.
O the magic pipes of Pan!

ATAVISM

In taste the sweat of fear is kin
To rage's salt, adrenalin.
In salty floods the sperm's relief
Flows bitter as the tears of grief.
In sorrow, love, in fear and bliss,
Wherever keenest living is,
Our glands in stress must always vent
An atavistic element
And pour across the temporal dam
Such seas as those our fathers swam.

So then in part our bodies leave
To join our finny Adam-Eve
Deep in their primal paradise
Salt-washed beneath its coral skies.

Since exercise calls from the deep
Abilities in us that sleep
Upon Life's dry and strenuous stage,
How much of passion, fear and rage
Before the weak-lunged actor, Man,
Becomes a full amphibian?

DIALECTIC

I bear a god within the brain
that beasts know nothing of
It makes me give against the grain
in the very name of love

By it the infant and the old,
the halt, diseased, insane
are kept from violence, hunger, cold
that in the beast-world reign

But I at best am centaur still,
god-vision trapped in flesh,
my selfish heart defeats my will,
my mindless loins unleash

Now in the haunts of passion slain
its flesh become a clod
the beast is sleeping, and in its brain
revives the fallen god

STATEMENT OF METAMORPHOSIS

. . . a caterpillar
heavy-footed crawls
up the green-stemmed earth
weaves chitin walls

of patterned shape
encased in bone
rigid as cast
and hard as stone

Through freezing calm
and hammering storm
the chrysalis
retains its form

but life unfulfilled
there dynamis is
working its own
metamorphosis

Slow the free dream
takes shape in pain
strong self fingers
the gross flesh strain

torture and twist
at their patient task
till the earth-bound grub
under the mask

sloughs off the dead shell
of its useless lair
crawling on light wings
up the blue-stemmed air . . . .

STILL

though quazars pierce an emptiness
six billion light years cannot hold

though light itself is trapped
in the cold of collapsed nebulae

though all of history
is dwarfed by spatial sands

still . . .

the earthworm glistens in the dew
its beauty independent of
the hunger of a bird

USORTITOUT POEM

When they say, I love you,
What do they mean?

(dog)	(wants to win over)	(a mirror-image)
(God)	(wants to gnaw)	(lobster)
(politician)	(wants to save)	(ice-cream)
(gourmet)	(wants to sleep with)	(a bone)
(child)	(wants to protect)	(daughter)
(mother)	(wants to eat)	(mistress)
(ego)	(wants to worship)	(the electorate)
(lover)	(wants to lick)	(mankind)

OVERLOAD

these modern-day prophets
speak to the young,
*Be open, expand
your mind, receive, send*

is it any wonder
that the young crack up?

do you know
how many trillions
of impressions
bombard each of us
on every conceivable
wavelength
during the psychic
energy
of a lifetime?

how to shut off
the screaming overload
how to handle
it in patterns
how to restrain
from adding to
the cacophony
these are essential
tricks for survival
and must be learned
early

whether or not
we like it
we are caught between
monitor and madness

I SHALL NOT WHEN I DIE

I shall not when I die
Quake for hell-fire
Nor dream with desire
Of a celestial sky,

But rather grieve with pain —
Still thinking on
The things I have done
And may not do again.

THE LACK

No man has felt a keener sting
Nor known a lack so strong
As he who has the urge to sing
Without the gift of song.

REALITY MYTH

Every man who saw her
grew lust-mad
and tried to seize her
but her legs
were swift arrows
none ever caught her

And every woman
was panic-stung
by her perfection
With cries and clubs
the women drove her
from the house of living

To the kind
and simple children
she never was
and all the animals
pressed noses to the ground
too near to see her

On the day
she vanished
only the birds
worried the sky
with the troubled grief
of their throats

Memory's cloud
over a sun
can filter a blaze
into a round
and maneagable
mind-disc

Sometimes now
a man remembers
and his lust turns love

as he searches
through shoals of women
for her trace

And sometimes too
some woman's recollection
draws her to look
for the friend
she might have had
and never did

But it is all vain
for no one knows
what it was ever
became of her
and grieving birds
still trouble the sky

FARMER

In summer time my true love cried,
"Come, spend your days with me!"
But I heard the call òf untilled fields
And I left her angrily.

Here in the field the days are dull
With rain, and mist and cloud:
It matters not how heavy-ripe
My corn awaits its shroud.

HAIKU

coin-silver on a
dark rich tablecloth, who will
pick you up, full moon?

A PATHETIC FALLACY

. . . the staccato rain
that hammers on the pane,
the lightning-flash,
the thunder-crash
as our frantic flesh
struggles to unleash
its pent-up stress
of loneliness
and grind it down
to full oblivion
in the mindless swarm
of nature's storm . . .

INVISIBLE GLASS

the first time his father hit him
he felt enveloped in a spun-glass world
in which time was nowhere
and all that happened never was
once the glass was gone and he
became himself again

and every time that precious self
he polished like a shining coin
was threatened, glass came back
to shield him, shut him off
from any direct touch
of disharmonious universe

the night he turned the chevvy over
the day his cheating was found out
the time he ratted on a friend
sufficient armour
against a one-shot threat
glass kept reality at bay

but hooked by a habitual danger
to self-esteem he found
the glass grow thick and tight
it anaesthetized all feeling
and in his sober state
refused to go away

you'll find him in a bar-room now
with a glass gripped in his hand
the only antidote he knows
to that invisible globe
in which his bottled self
is caught and held

QUALITY

I tell myself
we are all robots
that what and where
our program centres are
in our only difference

programmed to pleasure
whose nexus lies
in outer stimuli
I respond to the world
through which I move

but when I am loved
by a being who draws
passion and power
out of her own
inner essence

light from such a source
opens a third eye
by which I know with pain
some patterns are real
others facsimile

CONTIGUITIES

I

yap	pay
on	no
sore	eros
live	evil
dog	god

II

rats	star
are	era
now	won
&	&

evil	live
drawer	reward
saw	was
drib	bird
&	&
drab	bard

THE SKELETON THOUGHT

Ever to destroy
My feasts of joy
This skeleton thought
Creeps in unsought
That all who've quaffed
Life's champagne draught
O'erbrimming poured
Have come to hoard
The weak cold tea
Of memory
Their cracked cups hold
As though 'twere gold.

LOVE EPISTLE

Sweet, had I loved in Herrick's golden time,
My love had anguished on the rack of rhyme
Long years to make my laggard tongue confess
Fresh heresies upon your loveliness,
And bind with dogmas what no words can bind,
The largesse of your body and your mind.

And so, my dear, since courtly days are done
And love asks now no cleverness from one
But lets the other willing members try
That task was once the tongue's monopoly,
Let straight the free-verse tributes to you rise,
Writ by the willing pupils of my eyes,
And let your heart with mine beat sarabands
In joined electric pulses of our hands,
Till, moved by mutual rhythms in the head,
Our lips, both yours and mine, wax melting red,
Shall print upon the parchment air between
One single image of the song they mean.

And when each part of each has had its share
Of word-transcending joy, then let us dare
Love's death, that silent song which doth eclipse
All works of tongue and eyes and hands and lips
To flame, our phoenix triumph over Time.
O let us die together in one rhyme!

RESPONSE

see, jubilantly
round and round on tether-twigs
circling leaf-wings fly

and a lark folds wings
out of the wind and perches;
still while the tree sings . . .

A CRITICAL REVIEW IN VERSE

When strong his adolescent urges press
A little boy must brag his naughtiness
And show with pride upon the public shelf
The naked parts of all his shameful self
While other lads who keep the dread taboo
Stand by and thrill to deeds they dare not do.
But though anticipation makes them quake
Neither the sky nor its foundations shake.

So these poets write, whose hearts still glow
Through perverse fogs of cloudy libido;
With "goddams" scattered through their verses rough,
Like boys they curse to show the world they're tough,
Or rape in slow and dreamy metaphor
The fancied virgins whom they dare not whore,
Then wax ecstatic over thighs and knees
Like peeping Toms who see their first strip-tease,
While critics in their magazines rehearse
The praise of all who dare to sin--in verse:
So hard they try to show us what we've missed
You'd think that none but they had ever kissed.

But when these circles of the brash and young
Have done their best at *Contact* and *Combustion*,
They'll find their efforts have not changed at all
The clods that form the cold Canadian wall.

MY DREAMS I ENJOYED

My dreams I enjoyed
Until I read Freud
And learned that their flow
Leaked from a Libido
Whose urge is excessive.
Now I'm manic depressive.

SMILING TOM

When you saw me you smiled like a pulsing red sun
That thawed out my heart and made my blood run,
And I wished that its light would never be done
    When you smiled on me, Smiling Tom.

It was with your smile that you wooed me and won
When you met me down by the blackberry run,
But you smiled, too, when blackberry days were done,
    And you said you would leave me, Tom.

Your smile was as gay as it ever had been
When you said good-bye to me there on the green.
'Twas a knife in my breast as sharp and as keen
    As this knife in my hand, Smiling Tom.

But you smiled your last smile when you turned to be gone.
In the cold damp bed where you lie alone
No smile breaks out on the white smooth bone,
    Not even your own, Smiling Tom.

ACCEPTANCE

Like a caterpillar
Pursuing its fellows' thread
Around a saucer's rim
No more my thoughts traverse
The circle grooved by myriad minds
Skirting mystery mountains.

Here in my narrow valley
I shall sit at ease
And eat the wholesome fruit,
Knowing all roads escaping
Turn backwards on themselves.

A RESPECT: FOR A POET

When he is dead at last
do not remember what he did
and say, In this he was good
or wise, That sin in him was hid

deeds find a way to sink
down time's dissolving sea
that drowns both bad and good
all bodies and their memory

say rather, He carved poems
from the liquid hours that ran
and froze epiphanies
in words that all who read can scan

THE LONELY ONES

Locked in their roles by pride
The lonely ones go by;
Disguised, like us they hide
In their conformity.

Desire and duty war
In every routine move;
So all alone they are,
So much they long for love,

That secret hiding place
Wherein the magic lives
Whose flesh-strokes can erase
The world's imperatives,

Whose quick touch leads to soul
And ends all masquerade
In the merged world that all
Who love in truth have made.

About us everywhere
The lonely ones still move;
So all alone they are,
So much they long for love....

IN THESE PHRASES CAUGHT

I

in these phrases caught
snowflakes on dark ebony
stars in a night sky

merge, swim minuscule
goldfish in the riffled pool
of your fluid thought

II

ask not why or how
I a poet sent them so
thought-waves of sight-sound

true to its own ring
while it's struck will a bell sing
deep out of its wound

FULL CIRCLE

A little boy holds one end of a string.
The other end is tied to his pulltoy.
The pulltoy's wheels rest on the grass.
The grass is rooted to the earth.
The earth touches the water of the sea.
The sunlight strikes the water and draws it up.
The water vaporized becomes a cloud.
The cloud bursts and falls as rain.
The rain falls on the little boy holding a string.

OVER THIS COLLECTED SELF

that crawling baby, that spoiled child
exploding temper-tantrums
and that adolescent swagger
masking fear or guilt
your mind suppresses

over this collected self
a conscious you as master
proclaims that even if
such beings once were there
they now no longer are

but as it does, your body turns
to seek a foetal posture
as stimulant to sleep

VALLEY-SLEEPER

from the French of Arthur Rimbaud

There is a green glade where a cool stream purls
And madly catches grass for silver rags,
Where the sun shines above the haughty crags:
A tiny vale a-foam with light that swirls.

A soldier-boy, open-mouthed with unbound curls,
Neck-deep in blue iris lies fast asleep;
Pale in his green bed where the light-rays weep
He lies on grass; above him a high cloud whirls.

Like a sick child he smiles, and sleeps beside;
With feet in irises he takes his rest.
Cradle him warmly, Nature: he is chill.

The fragrance cannot tickle his nostril:
He sleeps in sunlight, one hand on his calm breast.
He has two red holes deep in his right side.

ACT OF LOVE

Although the space between us lies immense,
There floats across the void from him to me
The fine-spun gossamer of poetry
Drawn from the entrails of experience.

Not like a web that catches flies by chance
And lets them wither to oblivion;
This is an act of love whose touch is one
With all of mind and muscles' nervous dance.

A Trojan plain, the sound of martial drums,
A withered crone, face torn by grief and fear
Amid the press of Grecian victory.
No need to ask the question now: "What's he
To Hecuba that he should weep for her?"
I read, and in my tears the answer comes.

THERE ARE TWO WORLDS IN TIME

There are two worlds in time; one dark, one light:
In circling stasis each on other preys,
Where all between the poles of black and white
Revolve or spiral through their nights and days.

When you behold the blind and silent worm
Become a song inside a robin's throat,
Or see in Spring an orchid blossom form
Its own sweet scent from slime that feeds its root,

Think how in turn a worm will feed as well,
One night to come, upon that robin's meat,
Or how the root that gave will canniball
And care not if the bloom be foul or sweet;

And realize, then, unlike flower, worm, bird, slime,
Your thoughts of time have put you outside time.

L'AMOUR LA POESIE

from the French of Paul Elouard

So calm the gray, faint, scarred
And weak skin of night trapped in flowers of frost
She keeps only the forms of light.

As a lover, she is right to be beautiful
She does not await the Spring

Weariness, the dark, repose, and silence
A whole world living among dead stars
Trusting that things will last
She is always visible when she loves.

QUEEN STREET HOSPITAL

High ceiling with dark walls
Dwarfing arm-chair areas
Where patients for the most part
Drugged to lethargy
Meet relatives in a total
Absence of privacy.

The woman who was with me
Exchanged banalities
With her hopeless son
And an ugly girl beside us
Screamed curses at her father
For having brought her here.

Under the lights' electric glare
Strange shadows moved.
Mumbling some excuse
To save their feelings, I exited
To a blue-sky world
Of trees and summer sun.

To calm my nerves, I opened
That day's copy of the *Toronto Star.*
I can still see the headline,
What may indeed be loony truth
To end all lunacy:
HAPPINESS IS A THORNCREST FORD.

LOVE ON MY PART

Love on my part
Is sweet, absurd;
It makes my heart
A crazy bird

That now must sing
A springtime song
Though every Spring
Has come and gone.

Let it sing clear
Both night and day...
Its notes may scare
Time's chill away.

YOUR RIGHT EYE AND MY LEFT CONJOIN

Your right eye and my left conjoin
in a noble nice propriety:
my left in your right eye finds a twin
in its keen zest for deviltry.

not touching, eyes open, close we lie...
I'm left-handed, and right-handed you...
Let's each close up the weaker eye
and let our devils have their due.

THE BLINDMAN AT THE CONFERENCE

On an unfamiliar campus
The blindman at the conference
Depended on strangers

They never let him down

I have seen men walk beside him
Out of their way and in their busy time
While he explained to each in turn
That had he three weeks in the place
He would find his way alone

He asked me for directions
And as I strode beside him
Down the corridor, he said,
"People are so good to me
Because they know I'm blind."

I smiled to hide a sudden rage.

I am more blind than he
But dare not ask for help with trust like his.

FIRST AND LAST

..the Spring's first orchid
frail and pink amid dead leaves
of chilly April

and Fall's last green leaf
clinging to a glassy twig
in cold November

are my familiars
who dare live life to the quick
against all weathers ...

WHEN MIND JUMPED THE VOID

When mind jumped the void
Between sounds and found symbols
A new arc-light blazed,

filling time and space
with flame.   As I write, its glow
sparks everywhere

a great mind-spectrum
from blue peace to scarlet rage,
Behold the marvel

and bless this word-world
in which the viewers and the
light they see are one.

PHAETON

All the years I hunted butterflies
In field and wood and lane
I saw but once a phaeton
Perched on a blue vervain.

Slow I crept up near as could be,
So tense I scarcely breathed,
Then swiftly swung my trusty net.
In gauze it was ensheathed.

It hung a score of years, the pride
Of my collection
Till time and parasites combined
For its destruction.

But I know now that while I live
I never shall forget
The intense and awful joy I felt
When I caught it in my net.

I'VE LITTLE PATIENCE WITH

I've little patience with those friends of mine
Who say that life is naught since all men die--
Who would the tavern's richest juice decline
Because the tavern closes bye and bye?

AGAINST THE LOVE VIRUS

against the love virus
he inoculated himself
by a long course in philandering

in his case, a cure
more deadly than disease

TWO MONARCHS

Caesar's coin
Is copper, silver, gold,
Melted out of solid rock
And minted in a compact space
To pass with ease from hand to hand.
Caesar's coin
in space and time is durable.
It is, of course, transferable.

Not so is God's.
It's wishes, thoughts, and deeds
Melted out of living loves
And minted from a dream that died.
Soul-currency in matter's paradigm,
Transcending time and space,
It cannot pass from hand to hand.
It cannot be defaced.

With such a wealth of either kind
We would indeed be fortunate
Were there not inside us still
Two monarchs at cross purposes.

A BOY WHO LOVED BIRDS

a boy who loved birds
could never coax them to him
nor join in their flight;

a boy who loved flowers
could not keep them from wilting
when the Fall frost came;

and when an auto
struck his dog, what could his love
do to make it well?

then he tried prayer
with all his heart, looked to heaven
and got no answer;

after that he knew
the world was indifferent
but he kept caring,

learning as he grew
not to live for power but
for feeling, being;

like other insects
in a giant universe
he went on his way,

alive in his self,
thanks to the dumb charity
of soil, sea, and sun...

DIDACTIC

Since I shall never have a son
I write these words for any one

Who for the first time knows the truth
That hides beneath the bloom of youth

To plumb an awful cavity
Between the *is* and *ought-to-be.*

This world that seems so fair behind
Its veil of seeming is a blind

Where things that should not be but are
Assail the nose, tongue, eye, and ear

And by their slow infection try
To make us inmates of its sty.

What then ought you to do? Decline
The challenge and go root with swine?

Or weep into your tavern beer
To mourn the fates that brought you here?

Or prematurely end the game
Whose dice are not the dice they claim?

Avoid such cop-outs, then, my son.
Do what I and better men have done.

Like you, both they and I saw through
The veil that blurs the false and true;

Saw, too, the world of grace and sin
As paradigm for ours within;

Saw in this power to know and see
The germ of inner victory

And built a citadel of self
With quality as basic wealth,

And from this base we outward strove
To aid the good we prized through love.

We faced grim foes that tried our grit;
Defeated oft, we never quit,

But raised our standards proud and high
Against all mediocrity

To learn beyond all bitterness
That winning, losing matter less.

It is the joy of battle-glow
That sets adrenalins aflow

And gives a tang and zest to life
That more than justifies the strife.

NOVEMBER 11, 1979

Now at the cenotaph
The recent marchers pause.
Bagpipe and brass are still.
Faint in the thin distance
A crow calls--hoarse reminder
There is no armistice in nature.

And in my mind's eye
I watch it all,
I who am at odds
With this a-historic century
(If *now* is all there is
Against what does one judge its flavour?)
Yet will not leave my room

To march in this parade
Or be physically a spectator.

In my upstairs study
Lies a pile of *Legionaires*,
Each issue louder, thicker groans
In silent type with names I know.
Each name denotes another gap
To shrink the dwindling file
Of gray-haired marchers
On each memorial day.

Remember how we used to think it fun to sing:
"Ninety-nine bottles hanging on the wall.
If one of those bottles should happen to fall
There'd be ninety-eight bottles hanging on the wall."

Though history may have its cunning passages
Whatsoever ways we twist and turn or march
Are ways that lead to one labyrinthian centre
Where the minotaur we face
Is known and recognized by us at last.

I recall a long-ago parade.
Grey, Scotch-mist. Sky overcast.
The company assembled in the square.
Stiff, alert, we stood and waited.

Our commander and three civilians came.
An old couple, shabby, thin, together with
A pale, pinched girl.
Down among our files they went
And paused before each man.

The girl with hopeless, hoping eyes
Would scan each face in turn, then turn away
With lowered head, and as they moved
A growing tension gripped our ranks,
Dispelled in titters when a wag
Cried out, "Pick him, Miss,"
And pointed to a quaking youth.

At last the thing was over
And all platoons dismissed intact.

Or so it seemed to me the day it happened.

I remember wondering why that wretched girl
Peered through our line-up as she did.
Was it to denounce a rape or pick
The father of an unborn child?
And if she had chosen me, or any
One of us, what could we have done or said?
And through it all I felt that first-time guilt
That is the basic heritage of man.

It did not then occur to me
That we, as much as she, were victims too,
And that the whole parade was allegory.

Men do not choose.

Since then, my comrades one by one,
Without their leave, are singled out.
I read their names and numbers
In The *Legionaire.*

Not for me the cenotaph,
The march, the bagpipe, brass.
Be mine that raven-voice, crying
Against a ceremonial lie,
There is no armistice in nature.

IT SEEMS INDEED A THING MOST ODD

It seems indeed a thing most odd
That man who deems himself to be
The very image of his god
Is yet blood brother to a flea.

215

ABOVE THE PURPLE HEATHER

Above the purple heather
A bird sang in the sky.
It is more than thirty years
Since last I saw it fly

It is more than thirty years
Since bird and song were dead,
But the notes it sang that day
Go trembling through my head.

Though it takes three thousand miles
To reach that heather hill
As I write my nostrils now
Draw in its honey-smell.

Above the Scottish heather
A lark its song set free:
All of it that lives is now
In Canada with me.

DOPPLEGANGER

walking a snowy sidewalk
one moonlit night I met myself
going the other way...

too late I saw who it was,
for when I turned to look
it was no longer there.

I stood depressed and shaken,
knowing I would not meet again
him whom most I wished to know.

HAD OUR LOVE'S DISEASE

Had our love's disease
Made but our own bad weather
I would have said, "Please,
Let us be ill together."

But this infection
Stops not at our own portal;
There are more than one
I fear will find it mortal.

Yet I'll not say, "Wait,
Make them all safe forever."
It is now too late;
Our souls have caught the fever.

MYSTERY

It is indeed a mystery
That one young and beautiful
Who can touch, taste, hear, see, and smell
And has more units in her skull
Than any spiral nebulae
Should find life dull

FOR AN ARTIST

for an artist
it is better
to be a well-placed
candle
than a blazing sun

to illuminate
without distortion
the empty spaces
between and around
what is normally seen

CONTENTS